Sunshine *Soldier*

A WW2 Combat Infantryman's Story

They call him "Sunshine" …a combat infantryman's story
With the fighting 79th Inf Div. and Eisenhower's SHAEF G2 Intelligence,
chronicles events for one teenage GI, 1943-1946, state training to Berlin,
a WW2 book. By Pfc. Harrison West,
42018762 Browning Automatic Rifleman Baker Co. 315th Inf. Regiment,
Fighting 79th Div., 16th Corps US 7th Army, ETO.

Harrison West

DEDICATION

To my loving and understanding wife, Nancy Winter West and my six children and twelve grandchildren, who have provided steadfast understanding, support and encouragement over the years in all of my WW2 projects and endeavors.

To my late dad and mother, Donald C. West Sr. and Oneita L. West, who held down the home front during the WW2 years, and, with uncommon dedication and persistence, managed, processed and distributed this enormous volume of primary source documents for Sunshine Soldier including war letters and other family archives all across the USA, and did so particularly during the 63 days straight I was on the line, continuously, at any given moment, not knowing if I was dead or alive.

To, my brother and his wife, Donald C. West Jr. and Wilma West, who safeguarded the above "Family Archive Time Capsule" for the approximately 40 years it resided in California.

© Harrison West 2020

ISBN: 978-1-09830036-4

CONTENTS

Chapter Twelve

Chapter Thirteen
Hospital evacuation train after wound… From 1st Battalion Aid Station and MASH through Besancon and Marseilles

Chapter Fourteen
Eisenhower's Military Intelligence Service (a whole new life at SHAEF MAIN HQ) 149

CHAPTER ONE

The early days, Lindy through schools and Purdue to Fort Dix

PREFACE REMARKS: The action timeline for chapters one to three covers the period 15 July 1925 to 19 November 1943. The primary source documents are war letters written 63 years ago. In the middle of the Roaring Twenties, Charles A. Lindberg, Lindy, ushers in the era of Modern Aviation with historic, first solo flight across the Atlantic Ocean in 1928. Mountains of snow land in Buffalo. First news of Pearl Harbor arrives in Westfield, New Jersey. I train on 105/155 mm howitzers at Purdue field artillery ROTC. And watch out for the hook! Fort Dix Induction Center.

Chapter One - Part A
Early days, school grade 4, 238 Avenue A Forest Hills, PA (vicinity Pittsburg) 'Lindy' and the Roaring Twenties in Smokey City! 1925-35

I enter this world 15 July 1925 in Wilkinsburg PA, between Pittsburgh and East Pittsburgh, second son of Donald Corbly and Oneita Leone Harrison West. Dad works as an electrical engineer at Westinghouse Electric Corp., and we live at 238 Ave. A, of the "Westinghouse Plan," in the community of Forest Hills, near Wilkinsburg.

It is an exciting time for kids to grow up, and my earliest memories are of my very first scooter, a universal treasure of kids too young and small for bikes. There are hills, some very steep, all over the plan, so our scooters are stout and built to be as safe as possible. My new scooter is big and blue, with big 12" wheels with an enormous, drum brake in the rear, easy to ride. We are brought up in regular Sunday school at the East End Christian Church of Pittsburgh.

The last years of the Roaring Twenties are dominated by Charles Lindberg's solo flight over the Atlantic in 1927, so the whole world is ga-ga over "Lindy"... especially the kids. No exception, I push my blue scooter up all of the local hills and then literally fly downhill, riding the brake all of the way. In keeping with the local dress code, I am sporting my snazzy leather, "Lindy" aviators cap and goggles, the open straps flapping in the wind.

To top it all off I have a neat 6" wind driven propeller mounted between scooter front forks. It spins with sustained splendor and determination. Now, Lindy himself didn't have much more! So, it is that I am launched into the excitement of aviation and aircraft engines... to be a lifelong focus in my life. My brother Don shares the excitement and we are both members of the "Sky Climbers Club" of Pittsburgh. This is our haven for supplies and support for building small, solid scale model airplanes of the day. No molded plastic. We sculpt them out of solid balsa wood and paint them with pride in bright colors.

In the summertime excitement abounds in two other highlights of my life: The ocean and Bay of Long Beach Island off the coast of New Jersey and the fabulous Cleveland Air Races. My folks had a Ford Model "T" which they replace in 1929 with a classy Marmon sedan. This featured a neat, mohair upholstered toolbox mounted high up above the rear seat, left side by the window. Just my size to my delight. I recall perching up on top of this comfy box to see all the sights.

No seat belts mind you (not invented yet) but what the heck... what else could a kid want. This is a time of poor metallurgy for rear axles in autos. They had a habit of breaking when brittle in the cold winters. This happens at least once with me perched on the toolbox as the family made our annual Christmas time tour of the beautiful Christmas lights in the hills of Mount Lebanon.

This is also the time prior to the Pennsylvania Turnpike (America's first Interstate), when low power, put-put, family cars have a tough time making it over the Allegheny Mountains on trips east. Our family prays mightily as we struggle in the Model T and Marmon to get over the summit of Mount Tuscarora on trips to the wonders of Spray Beach, NJ.

A decade later families easily zip through the mountains, not over them on what will become I-76. Finally arriving at Spray Beach my Dad, starting a family tradition, makes elaborate sand sculptures of motorboats and airplanes, outfitted with steering wheels and joysticks just made for tiny people. Kids from all up and down the beach line up by the dozen for their chance to sit in enticing seats and cockpits and make motor-like sounds. Unforgettable images sustained through to the next century as future West families build "Ball Roller's" and associated architecture on the beaches of Galveston, TX.

Home Base   Vicinity – Pittsburgh, PA   1931-35

This is notably the era of the historic Cleveland Air Races, of Col. Roscoe Turner and his bright yellow "Heinz 57 Special" and of Jimmy Doolittle (later of the Tokyo Air Raid fame) and his "GB Sportster" a stubby plane, all engine, almost impossible to fly. 5 years later, with the technology of the 21st Century, the Military/Wings Channel, brings this history to life for the new generations. Once or twice, from Pittsburgh and Buffalo Dad takes us to these fabulous air races: for me, life shaping events.

These Pylon Races with piston planes, flying short circuits at 2000 Indy speeds (220-230 mph) perhaps 40 feet off the ground can really stir one's blood. This is the "NASPLANE" circuit of the early Thirties cut short by WW2, not unlike the "NASCAR" circuit of the next Century. They persist in the 21st Century at Reno Nevada, including all kinds of classes including unlimited souped-up, WW2 PSl Mustangs. Something else!

Finally, the Roaring Twenties also closes with the 1929 stock market crash and the Great Depression. My folks pretty well keep me insulated from this nightmare as far as possible. Two related events in this regard touch my life:

In 1935 Westinghouse transfers my Dad to the Buffalo Regional Office, and then, in 1939 surpluses him along with a large group of Westinghouse employees who lose their jobs. The winds of war are now blowing so Dad finds a temporary job with the National Defense Power Commission in Washington, DC. And my brother and I complete our school years at Amherst Central High School (in the eastern suburbs of Buffalo) while Dad works alone in Washington. This saga ends happily when Charles Butcher, a Westinghouse friend and associate, is instrumental in finding Dad a permanent job as the Manager of the Research Lab for International Nickel, in Bayonne, NJ.

Chapter One - Part B
76 Fairlawn Drive, Amherst, NY (vicinity Buffalo), school
grades 5-8...mountains of snow for kids to shovel

We move to the eastern suburbs of Buffalo in the mid-Thirties and settle in a Spanish bungalow at 176 Fairlawn Drive, Eggertsville, NY. I attend 5th and 6th grade (Middle School) in Eggertsville and then 7th and 8th grade (Junior High), at Amherst Central High School, just a few blocks eastward.

Most impressive to me in this era is my brother Don Jr. 4 years older than I, graduating 12th grade when I was in the 8th grade. Swimming team coach Don also stars in the 'Pirate's and Penzance' operetta with movie star to-be, Jim Whitmore. Jim, a very stocky guy, is of course a key football hero.

After picking up a rental E flat alto saxophone and persisting with lessons for over a year my folks buy me a beautiful, 'gold' Conn Alto Sax for my birthday. This, and a short lesson series on the piano, start me on the music phase of my life, to be with me always. It starts me off with the Amherst High marching band and orchestra.

Of course, we frequent Niagara Falls, the home of Shredded Wheat, and the thunderous waters of the Horseshoe Falls. We attend regular Sunday School at the Amherst Unitarian Christian Church.

One Christmas I get my first bicycle, a beautiful, green Elgin with balloon tires. Following up on "Sky Climbers" of Pittsburgh I now peddle the few miles out to Buffalo Airport frequently. There is history in the making with the very first DC-3's in service. I get very close to these bright, shiny aluminum marvels that stir a kid's soul with the rumble of the massive radial engines.

State of the art of photography is in rapid advancement, peaking another lifelong interest. Saving "forever" I finally buy my first camera: a neat, folding Kodak Bantam, using 828 film (near 35mm). It is destined to go to war with me.

So, it is that our family moves for the last time from Buffalo to 227 Tuttle Parkway, Westfield, NJ. School grades 9-12 under the thunder of war. Here I complete my four years of High School.

CHAPTER TWO

Chapter Two– Part A
227 Tuttle Parkway, school grade 9

Here we live at 227 Tuttle Parkway, right across the street from Roosevelt Junior High School. To enter my 9th grade classes I roll out of bed and roll across the street to start learning... most convenient. We are also just a few blocks from the Westfield Methodist Christian Church, the YMCA swim pool, and the old Westfield High School.

Chapter Two - Part B
Through Senior High in Westfield, NJ. 1940-43. Between Plainfield & Newark, a prime commute village

While we still live at 227 Tuttle Parkway, we also check out the local commuter railroads. This is the era of the New Jersey Central commuter rail line. The line of huffing-puffing-smoke billowing, steam powered system with the old, quaint, squat "Saddleback" engines. We have only one car, so we run Dad down to the station in the morning and pick him up at night amidst much clanging, bells and whistles. These nostalgic days will prove to be of short duration. I often take this line into Elizabeth where it crosses the Pennsylvania Electrified line into Manhattan, New York City.

Here the Cortland St. area offers a vast array of specialty shops (electronics, radios, photo equipment, marine systems, etc.) one after another, side by side, all selling the same stuff. My technically inclined buddies and I were always in there on one project or another. In our Tuttle Parkway home, I build a darkroom and a "poor man's" enlarger out of a corn chips can, wood, and an ancient scrap lens. I also convert my tiny workbench (built for me by my Dad in Pittsburgh) into a tennis racket stringing bench, learn to play tennis at the Westfield Tennis Club and string rackets for members. These unending projects carry on through 1943.

Moving to the old Westfield High School for 10th through 12th grade several events shape my life. In a summer session I learn touch typing which literally was both to save my life in WW2 and to make possible writing nine books. I learn executive skills as President of the Mask and Mime club and officer of the school yearbook.

Perhaps standing out above all else I learn the joy and inspiration of music, both marching band and symphonic orchestra. Still playing my alto sax I am volunteered to carry the B flat baritone sax in the marching band… an unforgettable experience. One simply doesn't know the spirit of JP Sousa unless he marches and plays Sousa. That sax is bigger than I and gets pretty-darned heavy. On top of this, another life shaping experience comes in the symphonic orchestra. I get to play the bassoon part, on the barry sax, at the very bottom of the signature, cascading run in the Grand Canyon Suite which starts with the piccolo at the top. Absolutely unforgettable!

Chapter Two – Part C
How to best serve country: My future education

I am also blessed by a talented German teacher, Mr. Shaterian, we call "Shadrack," for two years he teaches us German by studying old German fables and reciting them in statewide contests. Unbeknownst to me at the time, this brief language familiarity is to have substantial impact on my life a few years hence. This comes in handy later, both in communicating with the people of Alsace Lorraine and in working with the 95% German speaking guys at Eisenhower's Shaef, G2 (intelligence) document section.

I am in the entrance hall of our 227 Tuttle Parkway home. December 7th 1941 when President Roosevelt's voice comes to us on the radio about the ''day of infamy''… Pearl harbor. Now my life really changes.

Near the end of my senior year at Westfield High I have to make the decision on how best to serve my country fighting for the survival of freedom and civilization itself, and hopefully still coming back home in one piece. Enlistment options directly out of high school cross my mind… The air corps or the navy. But these are effectively squashed by my near-sighted glasses. In any event, having indeed lived through it and studied the horrendous stories of survival on land, at sea or in the air, I am convinced there is no such thing as a "safer" service. In all three services, from ball turret gunners, P47 pilots, and Navy, aircraft carrier sailors, to the dog-face Army infantry, can get shredded, blown apart, fried alive in burning oil, and/or drowned with equal ease. It is a matter of duty and honor.

I also have to think about my future education. I want desperately to be accepted by Purdue University in Indiana after the war. Living in New Jersey this means limited "out-of-state" problems in entering Indiana schools. My high school records and credentials are excellent. The teachers of Westfield

High School really go to bat for me. Unlike many unionized teachers of the 21st century, the 1941-43 teachers at Westfield high school really know how to inspire and teach math, science, chemistry and physics along with the verbal skills.

So, in the end, I elect to gain acceptance to the upcoming, 16-week summer session at Purdue, starting in May 1943, and then wait for draft induction into the army. This way I am locked into Purdue with assured re-entry after the war. My teachers and faculty at Westfield High are solidly behind me on this. In unprecedented fashion they let me "graduate" a full month early, skipping final exams... The whole bit.

CHAPTER THREE

Chapter Three – Part A
150 Littleton Drive, W. Lafayette, Ind.Purdue Engineering School - it is off to Purdue!

May of 1943: on 24 Sept. I inaugurate my TOMLINE (Transcontinental and Overseas Mail) service in family communications. This in a letter to my folks in New Jersey, Grammy West in Kansas, and brother Don Jr. in San Francisco.

Dateline: **May-Sep.43, Michael Golden Shops, and Mechanical Engineering (ME) Buildings.**

Outfitted in a military "suntan" uniform I arrive at the Purdue Armory for my first session, course, and start gun drills on loading standard 105mm and 155mm Howitzers. The 105mm projectiles are self-contained including both the explosive shell and propulsion powder MIL ROTC training course and start gun drills in one giant cartridge. In the bigger 155mm projectiles we have to load the shell first, and then stuff in the propulsion powder bags, just like in the big Navy guns. This way one can tailor the shot for longer or shorter range.

The "ratio" of women to men on the Purdue campus is "slightly" in favor of the gals! Would you believe about 5 to 1... a clearly revolting development. It is amusing to watch (some) of these gals operate. They think they are right smart and hot stuff, and the sad part about this is that some, (like Pink the Wink), most assuredly are! What chance has a guy got? But who am I kidding and who has time to socialize? By far my biggest classroom and homework demand is with Analytic Geometry. With two classes per day I start the day with "Analyst" class at 8:00 am and end it with the same at 4:00 -4:50 pm. I have 25 minutes before dinner to study, and then do Analyst homework through the wee hours after dinner! I hit the dorm (sleeping bunks) signing up for 5:45 am PO (pull out by the call boy) the next morning.

Chapter Three – Part B
The Academic Load... Analytical Geometry

Some of this Analyst stuff is really beyond me... for instance, the equations for screw spring curves in 3 to 6 dimensions. Try that one for size! Alas the plight of budding Mechanical Engineers.

Draft Board Status:

It is now September 15 and I get my 1-A classification at the Indianapolis Draft Board. This starts the ball rolling. At the end of my 16-week term at Purdue I'll be classified as an Engineer and the ME School handles all subsequent relations with the Draft Board. They fully understand that every student wants to get as much college in as possible before he gets in classified as a Mechanical in the Army. I am still considering all of the pros and cons if I elect to transfer my files back to my home Draft Board in New Jersey. My Induction Call arrives on 15 October, and Friday, 29 Oct. 1943 at 5:08 pm I leave Indianapolis and arrive Newark the next morning. So, look out Army... here I come!

Chapter Three – Part C
Michael Golden Shops Basic "Hands On" Training

In WW2 days Purdue still teaches freshman engineers the basic manufacturing processes, hands on. This includes the hot process laboratories we call the "Heat 'em up and Beat 'em up" Course. This is in four sections: Arc Welding, Gas Welding, Heat Treating, and the Forge Shop. They also cover the Casting Foundry where we sand cast aluminum boat propellers and the Machine Shop where we make screws on automatic screw machines and turn aluminum cups on standard lathes. This brief encounter is to be invaluable to me in a future, 41-year career, designing aircraft engines (jets and turbofans) for General Electric in Cincinnati, Ohio.

This 16-week summer session is also crammed with all of the standard, freshman, Mechanical Engineering academics, from Analytic Geometry to Mechanical Drawing. On a typical day, at my room in Carey Hall I awaken at about 0600 to the sounds of the Navy V-12 student sailors doing close order drill in the quadrangle lawn. The campus is also swarming with Marines and Army ASTP (Army Specialized Training Program) active duty soldiers in training at Purdue.

Chapter Three - Part D
Fort Dix Induction Center, Newark, NJ.
Fort Dix Physical Exam Center, You're in the Army now. Watch out for the hook!!!

(Hypo needle). Pre-Induction Physical Exam Center, Newark, NJ. 29 Oct – 19 Nov 1943 Horrors of eye exam and Neuropsychiatrist then a 19-day furlough!

Beyond any doubt Brother West is now on the roll of the Enlisted Reserve Corps of the US Army, to be called to active duty on the 19 Nov.1943. Today, 29 Oct. we go through the Pre Induction Physical Exam in a massive, castle like armory in the middle of Newark. It is one mass of organized machinery... as is expected when the entire population of the USA (not about half of the population as in 2005, post the 9/11, our second Pearl Harbor) is fighting for its life and the survival of freedom and civilization. First, they put us through the teeth and eye tests before the major physical. It goes something like this: Some dull tool has already robbed me of my glasses. The old boy sits me down and asks, "What can you see on that on that eye chart on the wall?" I come back "not a darn thing." Next is the shrink! Clearly, trained by *Miracle on 34th Street.*

CHAPTER FOUR

Transport Overseas: New York City POE to Bayonne, France. Home of the Fighting 79th Combat INF. DIV.

P REFACE REMARKS: The action timeline for this chapter covers the period 28 August - 2 Oct. 44. The primary source documents are war letters written 63 years ago. WW2 is raging everywhere. The USA and it allies are fighting for survival in the midst of the most cataclysmic event in the history of mankind. It is to cost 50 million lives, at an average kill rate of 23,000 lives per day, for 2190 consecutive days. This... is the price of your freedom today. Survival of our civilization and freedom are at stake. On June 6, 1944 the Allied Forces attacked German forces on the coast of Normandy, France and gained a victory that became the turning point for World War II in Europe. This is known as "D-day". For the timeline of this book, it is now 2.5 months after D-day.

Chapter Four - Part A
Our Rail Trip: Fort Meade to Embarkation at NYC passing
a microcosm of American humanity trackside
Dateline: **28 Aug. 1944, 87th Div., Fort Jackson, SC, Ship-out Orders to Meade**
After a month of rumors, it was now for real. For the uninitiated, here is a snapshot of what Army orders look like: "The following named EM (enlisted men, including this soldier MOS 745 (Military Occupational Specialty - Rifleman) fr orgns indicated are trfd in gr (transferred in gear) to AFG Rep) Depot #1 Ft GG Meade Md are rationed (fed) last at this stat to include breakfast meal 29 Aug. 44 will report on 29 Aug. Will depart this stat 1201 (just after midnight) by rail 28 Aug Eff date of change on MIR (Morning Report) 30 Aug."

13

So, the die is cast heading this correspondent for the combat hardened 79th Div. in France as a replacement. Brig Gen. Colin, 87th Div. CO, gave us the straight scoop. We are not going on Louisiana Maneuvers. The 26th Div. just left Jackson on alert. The 87th Div. will follow in about a month.

It is a crisp Fall morning as our swift, silent, electrified troop train clicks its way along the rails and overhead power lines into the busy metropolis of the New York City Port of Embarkation (POE). Overhead our spring-loaded pantograph is singing its way under the power lines collecting the power we need.

At the Fort Meade POR (Port of Replacement) we entrained early this morning in a very precise manner. Hours beforehand, each soldier knew exactly where each item of his equipment was to be placed. Now it is for real and we all know it. On board the train is an unforgettable vision; an impressive line-up of "Bendix Aviation" steel helmets, row after row. Under each is a silent soldier, efficient when there is 'doing' to be done. Each mind is thinking thoughts of the things they used to do in the Country they are about to leave in order to save it.

These are boys, young and old from all walks of life. Boys from the Quartermaster and the Air Corps who are about to become combat GI's overnight and learn how to load a rifle the next morning. These, along with all the guys like this correspondent who had been thoroughly trained. Together now, we are the Infantry Troops of the US Army!

Burned into this correspondent's soul are the faces and the sights and sounds to be seen and heard by all of us, out the windows along gleaming rail right away on both sides of the track. It is an unforgettable microcosm of American humanity. Close by on our right, a huddle of bobbing heads in a hot dice game.

Here, lively factory windows chock full of waving arms and hats…these guys know we are a troop train, going off to a war in which their Country is fighting for survival. They see them most every day and keep a lookout for them. There, the weathered old face of a warehouse watchman… his head and handheld high his fingers in the sign of a "V" for victory. The eager, jubilant look in his eyes shall reside in my brain forever.

At this very moment Operation Market Garden, the Allied airborne assault in Holland is underway. The 315th Infantry Reg. of the 79th Division, which I am to join within a month, has fought its way to Einvaux France WV 0189 Nord deGuerre Zone on its way to Luneville. In the Pacific theater, our valiant Marines are invading the Japanese held islands of Morotai and Paulaus.

Everywhere, Coca-Cola signs bedeck the city walls. Then, our last glimpse of all that is the United States as our Troop Train glides on. On our left, a kid of the brat age hanging out a window, a tin hat on his head. Pa was at the window too! "Gee! I wanna be a soldier too!" Our windows are open and over the ensuing clickety-clack along the rails we can hear the reverberating strains of humanity shaking the train roof. All senses are in play. A fella by the name of Wess chimes in: "Ya know Westy... this situation grows more serious by the minute. I'm beginning to think we might be going overseas." As our fabulous train ride clicks to a halt near the POE dockside, we are both left with resounding thought. "Wow is this America? Is this USA a great Country or what???" Folks of the 21st Century would do well to take note.

Chapter Four - Part B
Live ammo training just to wake us up!
Dateline: **Tuesday 22 August 1944 - The hinterlands of Fort Jackson,**

No rest for the soldier. By brief orientation, the Infantry Battalion (our 3rd Bo. companies I, K, L and M) consists of 35 officers and 836 EM. Maneuvering to attack with supporting artillery, etc. it is a 1000-man strong fighting unit, requiring a high degree of teamwork, detailed S2 intelligence, S3 operations planning, command and control. After moving up silently and tactically in the wee hours it is now 0530 hours, and we find ourselves just behind the LD (line of departure). H hour (attack start) is 0630. At H minus 45 live 105mm howitzers (4.1 in) and 81mm mortars (3.2 in., smooth bores) begin whistling overhead like express trains in salvos of four.

At 0630 we cross the LD. Each rifleman with 64 rounds (8 clips) of live ammo, and each BAR team with 420 rounds (21 magazines @ 7 magazines each). Each GI in this three-man BAR team is carrying about 35 pounds of gun and ammo into combat. You young folks of the 21st century, pick this up and try running around with this load and see how far you get! Company M heavy weapons guys are carrying belt after belt of ammo for their light and heavy MG's (machine guns). The attack is carried out through well over 3000 yards (1.7 miles) taking hill after hill after hill. It is to be the loudest dang racket I ever did hear!

That is until the dark hours of 15 Jan.1945 that darn near killed me in Reipertswiller in the northern Vosges mountains. The live fire artillery, mortar and MG didn't keep any too far in front of us (in fact it was too darn close). The sound of the 105mm salvos rocketing and swishing overhead is really quite reassuring a solid base for the feeling that you have a strong arm helping you out. The plunging (enfilading) heavy, water-cooled MG tracer fire, overhead from the rear, chewing up the ground just ahead is a horse of a different color!!! Nerve racking doesn't even begin to describe it! There is the indescribable, ear splitting, stuttering and cracking and never knowing just how high it is just above our heads. That is until we actually see the plunging tracers right in front of us. At one point we are on final approach to the military crest of a hill upon which tons of MG ammo is plunging.

Infantry GI's have to put even more profound trust in those the guys aiming those MG's. On a lively hill in Lorraine in November, I am to be put to the ultimate test of trust... tracer fire from the rear... but not overhead. It is at waist level left and right... streaks of fire. This is the price of freedom.

Chapter Four – Part C
Logistics at the POR & Embarking at POE
Dateline: **31 Aug. 1944 - Our eastern Port of Replacement (POR)**

Fort Meade is a "Port of Replacement" - a section of this military reservation being occupied by the American Ground Forces Replacement Depot (AGFRD) No. 1. AGFRD No. 2 is on the Pacific Coast. A POR is something like an advanced reception center in that large numbers of troops are being transported in and out of it continually. No one group stays longer than a week or two.

The purpose of the POR is to evaluate every piece of a soldier's equipment and usually replace about 90% of it with brand new stuff. With certain items of new and improved design there are short cycles of specialized training on the new features and functions. "Most" new equipment includes full field packs (and brother, I mean full) and duffle bags. From the POR the GI's are sent to the POE (Port of Embarkation) … the last step before the big boat trip over choppy seas. My first brand new M-1 rifle... An indescribable experience. I hate to admit it, but a degree of pure GI has crept into my bones and blood. This in the form of being issued for my personal affection a brand new, class one, first string, high grade, US Rifle, 30 cal., M-1. It makes that blunderbuss I was shooting at Jackson look like something the cat drug in!

The new M-1 is full of minor, subtle improvements including an easier, smoother main spring. The manufacturer is Springfield, rather than Winchester, as in Jackson. We also were issued brand new M-3 service gas masks, about half the size and weight of the old mask; a big improvement over the old, good-for-nothing, neck tearing, hunk-a-lead design.

Included in our new equipment is a new infantry pack, copied and improved from the German design. It is a "variable geometry" convertible design. It can be configured into four different types of packs: Light Combat, Full Field, Embarkation-Short, and Embarkation-Full. The latter will stagger a self-respecting mule. The thing is positively huge! We call it the ol' Mule-buster!

Chapter Four - Part D
Ocean crossing, unescorted, on troop ship. Our
embarkation- boarding the RMS Mauretania
Dateline: **Wednesday 20 September 1944 - our last moments on USA soil**

It is a crisp dank day as we de-train, fall into boarding formation and file up to the loading officers at the dock entry point. Soldiers go up the gangplank one at a time... an Indian blanket draped over one shoulder, a big bag on the other hand a 90 pound "Papoose" on both. We are all decked out in a two-ton tin hat. Each guy stops at the foot of the gangplank where an "angel" Red Cross gal daintily stuffs five doughnuts in his mouth. A second gal rams them down with a howitzer swab rod, and a third gal empties a quart of hot coffee down his gullet. Is this a great way to board a troop ship or what???

Honeymoon over, reality sets in. An MP gives each typical GI a hefty boot, and the poor guy struggles and stumbles up the gangplank, almost bent to the knees with the humongous load, but quite happy when he makes it to the top. Here we are led by a loading officer through a series of passageways, up and down gangways, until we finally reach what is to be our quarters during the voyage. It used to be a swank barroom with marble top tables. Now it is Mess Hall No.2. The deal wasn't too hot but could have been worse. 99% of the floor space is occupied by plank tables and benches.

Chapter Four - Part E
The Battle of the Atlantic

The Battle of the Atlantic is one of the corollary stories which must be noted here for the education of most Americans of the 21st Century. This group tends to be absolutely clueless on the price actually already paid for their freedom today. This is the saga of the men who designed and built the incredible WW2 Merchant Fleet, and of those Merchant Mariners who sailed them with courage and sacrifice.

It is also the story of how this soldier correspondent got across the Atlantic safely when I could just as easily have wound up in one of the 1,614 ships sent to the bottom of the ocean! This, along with the 10,614 valiant Mariners and Armed Guards ending the war for them...forever. This does not even count the hapless military soldiers being transported onboard! They also went down with these ships. Just look at a video clip of just one of these ships going down with all hands lost. Then ask yourself why are millions bitching about the events of today? And whether or not the pitifully small current casualty rate is a price worth paying for the freedom of our grandkids.

Chapter Four - Part F
The Grand Lady, Atlantic Ocean liners of the Thirties
Dateline: **23 Sept. 1944 - Aboard RMS Mauretania (2), somewhere in mid-Atlantic for the S day trip dodging German U-Boats which can't catch us…** *we are too fast!*

To set the stage for the story about to unfold here it is appropriate that we back up the timeline a bit to September 1939 in New York harbor. Here no less than four Grand Ladies were laid up awaiting the end of the political crisis in Europe. This includes: The 81,000-ton RMS Queen Mary; The 79,000-ton Normandy; The 80,000 plus ton II de France; and the 36,000-ton RMS Mauretania christened in July 1938. It was a brief stay, as WW2 broke out. By March 1940 these were joined by a fifth, Grand Lady, 84,000-ton RMS Queen Elizabeth. All five were refitted as troop ships in Sydney and Singapore.

Together, this Grand Lady, WW2 Fleet transported an enormous number of troops in all directions over the oceans. During WW2 the Mauretania (2), the smallest Grand Lady alone. transported 350,000 troops, this correspondent included, over 540,000 miles. Just imagine what the whole Fleet did.

It also moved fast with 42,000 horsepower pushing 36,000 tons to 26.S mph at a staggering kinetic energy. And this was the *slowest* of the Grand Lady Fleet. The RMS Queen Mary captured the Blue Ribbon, crossing time award for good in March 1937 at 31.6 knots (36.4 mph). Hitler tried mightily to touch her, offered $250,000 and the Iron Cross to the U-Boat that could sink her. He failed and could never touch any of the grand ladies. Queen Mary also captured the single trip, single load record of 16,683 troops. Dodging German U-Boats that can't catch us!

Chapter Four - Part G
An Atlantic dawn on shipboard

With WW2 raging all over the world we find ourselves gently rolling in the warm sun in a sea which is calm beyond belief. Lollygagging in the sun my mind flashes back to my 7th and 8th grade days of 1937-8, in Amherst, New York. In the 7th grade, as any kid, I was fascinated by speed… particularly the speedometer on my brand-new Elgin bike. We used to race down the long, straight hill just south of our home. Pumping all out, it usually registered a max speed of 30 mph, and faster if "Briar," the huge dog was chasing us!

You have heard that tiny rocks (meteorites) out of space traveling at enormous speeds, can dig humongous craters in the earth. You have also heard that massive objects, like the 53,000-ton RMS Titanic, traveling relatively slowly at 22 knots (25.3 mph) can rip it's bottom off being stopped by a massive iceberg.

What do these three examples above (150 lbs. of kid and bicycle, a meteorite, and the Titanic) have in common? They are all governed by the equation Kinetic Energy (KE) =½ Mass x Velocity squared.

The last two examples achieve similar, enormous KE levels, but with reversed combinations of mass and velocity. I have not even had college physics yet at Purdue, so it is that I ponder these things while rolling gently on the deck of the RMS Mauretania on this sunny September afternoon. I just cannot imagine how this humongous ship could be plowing through the Atlantic at speeds comparable to my 150-pound bike race down Briar's hill... but it impresses the heck out of me. The 36,000-ton ship is not even being chased by Briar.

However, it *is* being chased by German submarine U-Boats, with entirely different motivations, speeds and power levels! It is my one fifth horsepower (+ gravity) bike versus 42,000 horsepower for the ship at comparable speeds. I also ponder how it is that speed is keeping us safe but have no numbers to make the case. Now, 63 years later... here are the facts: In WW2 the British Admiralty permitted ships capable of speeds over 15 knots (17.3 mph) to travel on their own as independents. Typical max speeds for German U Boats at the time were 7.3 knots (8.4mph) submerged on battery power, and 18.25 knots (21 mph) surfaced on diesel power. U-Boats traveling on the surface are very vulnerable, so our troop ship, the Mauretania cruising at 26.5 mph is three times faster than the submerged U-Boat.

Hence, we are safe! But now my attention is diverted to Betty Grable (top pin-up gal of the time) who is on the forward A Deck, in living technicolor. No GI can pass this up. After that I'll crawl back up on top of my nice soft mess table where I eat, sleep, work and write letters!

Dateline: Sun 24 Sept 44 -Aboard RMS Mauretania, eastern Atlantic

It is a grey dawn aboard this rolling ship that finds Mess #2 (cafeteria) an astonishing sight to say the least. Amidst the pervasive low rumble of the mighty steam turbines, gears and props all night, ghostly long-limbed forms wrapped in army blankets had tumbled to and fro with each roll of the ship. The seas were heavy, but below storm grade, and so guys only rarely rolled off of the tables. But they did wind up in some crazy, sawed off, pretzel positions with a leg sticking out here and there. The cooling night air was filled with incessant ratcheting and creaking within the ships structure, not all that old but clearly cyclically loaded, stress and strained. On the tables, off of the tables, on the floor, and on top of a 5 ft high stack of packs and bags, GI's begin to stir.

It is 0550 hours as a mass of GI's begin to poke around and out of blankets. Somehow the guys on top of the equipment stack hadn't rolled off. Mess tables clearly were not designed for 200 pounds of big GI's and "pack" pillows take the form of a swayback horse, bending at least an inch lower in the middle. Totally aside from the ships structure the tables themselves "editorialized" all night: they were bitching about the insult to their dignity with ominous squeaks and groans. With some hesitation I glance over at a hapless GI sleeping underneath one of these awful looking tables. He is still alive... but clearly under some residual mental stress. Our group has to get up very early to feed at the first sitting. Those darn lucky second and third sitting jokers sack out until 0900-1000 hours on real Navy bunks. Boo-hiss on them, bummer for us.

Typical Days on Shipboard:

While a majority of the enlisted men (EM) rarely do a darn thing all day long a few of us are caught in detail work sessions such as deck flooding and guard duty, temporary MP and deck police details. Four hours guard duty out on deck at night in that 25-30 mph icy spray is no fun at all.

KP Duty Aboard the Mauretania:

There must be at least 3000-4000 troops on board. That is a lot of guys to feed, and KP (kitchen police) duty is a real blast. Food in those infinite quantities is not so pretty when the old boat begins to bounce. We serve "sitting" after sitting as guys moved in and out hour after hour. We carry heavy, steaming pots in and out through the jam-packed, foul air, feeling like ambitious sardines swimming across to the other side of the can to visit. When the waves are high, food... hot sticky stuff, slops everywhere. One darn fool slops half a plate of strawberry jam in my hair. Talk about a bad hair day. I come back with a half-pot of hot coffee down his pants. Serves him right. After each sitting, we scrub down the tables, wash the pots and pans, mop down the decks, and then are trampled by the next group coming in. Anyone want to sign up for KP duty aboard a WW2 Troop Ship?

After the last sitting of the day each Mess Table becomes home HQ for four guys. So, every other night I sleep under the table. Several tables are piled 5 ft high with gear, packs, bags and helmets. Heavy load deflected the tables 4 inches in the middle. Every so often there is a terrible crash as the rocking of the boat tips over these pieces of junk. We are fortunate not to have a bad storm during the entire crossing although we do have several really rough days. Sea sickness shipboard is not a problem, though rock and roll loads are indeed bothersome.

The basic ship motion is up and down in an 8 second cycle. This is caused by the ship rocking on two axes. So, the "G" force on one's legs is in constant change from about 50 to 200 pounds. This is a real problem in "fighting" up the gangways, deck to deck, and then, a few seconds later, "literally float-ing" up and down the steps. Our home quarters were on B Deck, amid ship. For a 36,000 ton ship it is amazing to me that the helmsman had to wag the rudder back and forth all day to hold course! And we could feel it! Playing checkers on the mess tables, every so often we would awaken to the fact that we were putting up a terrific struggle to keep from sliding off of the bench. Real fun along with our games!

During morning inspection hours (1000-1200 hours) the officials kick all of the GI's up and out on the open decks. The deck levels run as orthodox from the keel, engine room, holds and crew quarters, up through Decks D, C, B, A, Main, Sun Deck, Officers Deck and the Bridge. The mass quantity of men staggers the imagination. Men are lying down on every square inch of open deck surface... horizontal to inclined plane. Once I stumbled around on top of guys stomachs, etc. for 45 minutes just to find an open spot where I could perch.

The ships PX (Post Exchange Store) sold a great variety of goods and very low prices if you wanted to sweat out a line that circled the deck four times. Life jackets with red night safety lights are worn constantly. Blackouts, absolute total blackout regulations, are a necessity and very, very strict. After darkness, getting out on deck is impossible! MP's standing at every gangway leading up to the decks are ready to start club beating on any GI who even looks like he wants a breath of fresh air! Night deck guards indicate to me that, on moonless nights, the total darkness up there is beyond belief. Even the general outline of figures cannot be distinguished at more than two yards. A one-foot range is necessary for face recognition. Speed alone won't keep this ship alive if some damn fool lights up just one cigarette!

Now hear this... remember the doughnuts? But, even speaking to those gals is a court-martial offense. Since this Soldier didn't want to get a court-martial, I of course, never speak to them. Also, I am clearly not the "operator" that is my buddy, Trevor Wilkinson. I am never even to see Trevor among the mass of GI's on this Mauretania. However, he must have been there, with his impeccable, incredible memory of all of the details. Later on, in 2003 on the Milwaukee DVD of the 315th Reg., 79th Div., he tells this tale. I leave it to the reader to decide whether or not to believe this guy. He says he was there and at the peak of operating efficiency. He swears he reconnoitered a secret route down through several decks, up forward a couple of miles, and back up through a mess of decks to where the Red Cross gals were! And all of this while passing a bevy of guards with clubs... pretty courageous guy, or he paid off the guards. Perhaps we will find out the name of some of the gals he talked to. I await breathlessly. Later on, in Chapter 6, you will hear how it was that Trevor and I shared the same pup tent in mid-October.

Chapter Four – Part H
Our last days shipboard on the Mauretania. Docking in Manchester, England
Dateline: **Sun 1 Oct. 44 - Aboard the Mauretania & in Liverpool -Manchester**

The sun going one way and the ship going the other way, we are royally shafted on the time deal. The evening hours evaporate down the drain. They keep dragging us out of the sack earlier and earlier. We do so much sleeping in the afternoon we can't get to sleep much before 2400 hours (midnight). Even with a life jacket as a pillow the steady throbbing drone of those powerful steam turbine engines and drive-train did not help any. The vibration is much greater than I expected... mostly low frequency gear grind and prop noise. A guy reading a newspaper would have trouble with the pages fluttering very noticeably. All you budding mechanical engineers out there, here is a fun fact to know and tell. Even though the ship is a massive 35,000 tons, this vibration response is what happens when you pump 42,000 shaft horsepower in to two props to drive the ship nearly 27 mph... to beat out the German U-Boats. I personally gladly take this safe speed margin any day to Hitler's U-Boats.

It is that lost hour between 2300 and 2400 hours that I do most of my thinking. This mostly about the improbability of my amazing status quo! It is 1 Oct.1944 and here I am, flat on my back at the foot of a huge movie screen, tranquilly gazing up at Betty Grable's "Coney Island" motion picture in living technicolor! My head is propped up on a comfy life jacket. And all of the above magic with bottomless fathoms of icy turbulent ocean below and all around me. All of this while the ship continues pounding away at the sea as it plows through the cold inky night. Is this an incredible adventure or what? I marvel and agonize at the awesome, huge, hungry looking wave knifed out of the sea by the incredible 23 knot plunging bow. And I contemplate which would be the more horrible fate? ...Being squeezed to death by a python or being pushed overboard?

This ship never stops to pick up any man... he is on his own. It is too dangerous for all of the rest on board. This is the face of war in the Battle of the Frigid North Atlantic. It is part of the price of our freedom today. Eventually this overgrown, water plowing machine had to stop churning. But, for a full six hours after I am on dry land that lousy boat didn't stop rocking! A persistent cuss.

Dateline: **Mon. 2 Oct. 44 debarking in the Liverpool-Manchester Harbor**

Churning minds... Read on. It is a heavy, dank cloudy sky that hangs over this Liverpool harbor as we enter silently. A cold, steady drizzle makes things even more depressing as we pull into the dock. It is 0300 hours in the middle of the night, mind you, that they drag all three to four thousand of us off the ship. But, no matter... we are darn glad to be there. The shrill blast of the odd looking, 3rd class rail troop coach awaiting us hurts our ears as it pierces the night air! The light rain turns into a pure English mist.

Angel Red Cross gals are there again... in the middle of the night, yet. Talk about accolades... they didn't have to be there, but they were, and it made a difference. More coffee and doughnuts... this time I got nine!

CHAPTER FIVE

Replacement camp outside Chester, England, UK.; Temporary home of the flood of American GI's heading for the fronts

PREFACE REMARKS: The action timeline for this chapter covers the period 2nd - 8th of October 1944. The primary source documents are war letters written 63 years ago. WW2 is raging everywhere. It is 3 months after D-Day Normandy.

Chapter Five - Part A
English troop train ride into Chester
Dateline: **Mon.2 Oct. 44, Vicinity of Liverpool, Manchester & Chester**

It is 0400 hours in a dockside English mist as the shrill whistle blast from the 3rd Class, classic Troop Train first captures our attention. We board the electrified train and start up more smoothly than the electrified "Pencey" trains in New York City, but with an amazing "Conga-Beat" from the smoke-stack, a kind of clickety-clack from the rails, soothing kind of "pendulum swing" to the coaches. The Brit coaches are divided into several separate compartments with no connecting aisle whatsoever. We suspect that the conductor swung on a rope from window to window on the outside to collect the tickets. As we stop temporarily at one suburb an elderly English gentleman eyed with the curiosity of a kid through the smoke curling from his pipe. We beckon him over to the window but were locked in visual stalemate... neither party knew what to say.

Then a bright corporal broke the ice with, "What's up Doc?"...an American vernacular approach to a cultured Englishman. This correspondent burst out laughing, and so does our subject of interest. Cooking on all four burners, as the saying goes, he comes back with a lively response string of free verse, paralleling our "Mares eat oats… song." Cute as heck, but in a strong dialect we just cannot handle. The censor cut it out, suspecting some kind of code. Amazing! This is in the dark, before dawn… quite an interlude at the face of war.

From the Liverpool dockside we now enter a patch of England about 25x35 miles, to the south east. This encompasses Liverpool and Manchester to the north, along with Chester and Northwich to the south. In the wee hours prior to dawn we find ourselves detraining in a small village near Chester. The intelligent crow of a rooster sounds off in the distance as our troop formation plays "hurry up and wait" on the platform. Our GI's are bent into a cold swirling wind. The first faint glow of light is stealing over the eastern sky. Then we move out on what turns out to be an hour long, 3-4 mile trek on a lonely country road… with the 85 pound "Mule-buster" packs on our backs. Our destination is an extensive US Military Reservation just few miles to the south, between Chester and Northwich. As a mammoth troop Replacement Depot it is a temporary home for the flood of American troops heading for the fronts.

Chapter Five - Part B
US Military Reservation & Replacement Depot – Our temporary home in England

This Bivouac Tent Camp was our Billet "hotel" for the flood of GI's constantly transiting through the area on their way to the war front.

Chapter Five - Part C
The English countryside; a vignette

It is 0500 when we set up camp & unload our packs in our new home, our first daybreak in England. Our hour-long march here is our first look at the English countryside and time to contemplate what is ahead for us. For the time being we set the war aside, as tourists in a foreign country with a natural curiosity of its way of life.

The motion picture short "Memphis Belle," a technicolor feature, is the story the B-17 of the same name and the vast layout of bomber bases in Britain. It displays incredulous panoramic views of the colorful English countryside… the doll like villages and farms, seemingly too green to be for real. The fact is I find it very real and even more so! Beyond belief! I must admit that my point of reference is of course the dull, grey, sandy, barren wasteland upon which most American Army bases are typically built. There follows my impressions during our hour-long hike along what seemed to be the longest winding road ever conceived in route to this camp.

Here we have small but well paved roads bordered by mounds of sod like earth topped by all manner of shrubbery, wild hollies dotted with red, hedges and berry bushes. Old and very beautiful trees stretch their mossy green limbs everywhere the eye turns. This abundance of green is fed by an almost continuous, yet intermittent, October rain most every day in this camp. This, as the warm Gulf Stream winds interacts with the swift, cold winds from the north, filling the entire countryside chock full with thick, green grass and other plants. It is the very first thing that hits one in the eye at first glance... everything is just so plain darn green. Did I mention that everything is green around here?

Here and there on both sides of the road are private homes of every description, all the way from very small farms to large wealthy estates. Even the smallest bungalow is neat and trim, most all with myriads of "Christmas Card" chimneys. It seems that most every house sports at least four chimney stack rectangular bases with two to four clay pipes sticking up out of each base. The English farmers take pride in the variety of ways they can cut off these pipes. The visual result is the "Candy Stick" houses in Disney cartoons. Built mostly of brick with white stucco inlays, sometimes bordered by dark timbers on the upper half. Occasionally a row of identical houses staggers up a hillside, each made remarkably individualistic with vivid colors and landscaping.

All shades of tile: red, orange, slate gray, yellow, white and blue are built into the overall pattern, everywhere. Maintaining their traditional privacy, the Brits have surrounded their homes with odd little fences, walls and hedges of all types. One very tidy farmer of modest means wove a stubby-like basket type fence around a colorful garden in his front yard. Everyone seems to do more than the best with what he has, and this is the hallmark of what this society has created here. The very wealthy estates are great of course, but not a fair overall judgment criteria on this wonderland southeast of Chester, England. Anyone with the means can spend millions and produce fantastic results… it is low budget innovation that really counts!

Chapter Five - Part D
Pass into the town of Northwich
Dateline: **Thursday 5 October 1944, "Any gum chum?" Northwich, 10 mi NE of US Depot. & 15 mi. ENE of Chester.**
Northwich is a quaint, fair sized town population near 35,000, about 10 miles to the north-east of our Replacement Depot camp and is our selected target for our late day pass into town. It is in a light cool mist amidst that delightful old peep-peep of the English locomotive that we detrain from our 8-man carriage we quickly become lost in a mob of GI's "gently" beating its way to the ticket takers gate at the end of the platform.

I am with a fella from my same training platoon at Fort Benning as we move forward down to the main drag. We are fortunate in having the last minutes of dusk by which to see the town, already closing its ports like a reluctant clam in prep for the standard WW2 "Dim-Out" (almost black-out) all through England.

All of us being chowhounds, our first priority was food... we had to skip chow at camp to make it to the train. We find our way along a narrow, winding, cobblestone street with the inevitable shops left and right. We pass one of the two cinemas (movie houses). Their modern construction sharply contrasts with the quaint old line of gabled roofs with those sawed off, dog leg, clay pipe, quadruplet chimney stacks. The theater is playing "The Imposter" and "Gone with the Wind" was the coming attraction. By now hundreds of American GI's have control of the streets, with an occasional native couple here and there. Lively squads of youngsters roam the streets everywhere, averaging about 5-12 years in age.

Their incessant challenge to all of the GI's is "Any gum chum?" How about that... and in the cutest, inflected accent. The younger set over here have apparently become chewing gum addicts since the yanks started coming. They simply don't have the treat in England, and they crave it all the more. One little fella comes trotting up to me, his tiny hands gripping at the bottom of my combat jacket pockets. He insists I have gum. I insist I don't. "Iffen I hadda knowed" about it I "woulda hadda done brought" a whole carton from the States. Still the little kid persists... "All GI's have gum!" Talk about feeling like an absolute heel. Bummer. A tip to all forthcoming GI's ...always bring gum, soap and cigarettes etc. with you.

On another occasion a fella about 12 comes up to me with a more sophisticated approach. He has several USA coins and wants to trade them for Brit money so he can buy some candy. In total excitement he points to his grubby little hand, "Now here I have two nickels and three pennies US." I glance down. He actually has two quarters and three dimes. I point out the error and give him a half-crown, one and six pence in equivalent change (about 70 cents, US), and he walks away a very happy kid.

It has grown dark now as the full moon skips out into the clearing sky lighting up the ancient looking Northwich shops in striking hews. At a careless survey of the situation we felt anything but safe. It is plain eerie. Only faint cracks of light filtering out through slits in the dim-out curtains and blinds indicate the "pubs" and shops are open for business. It is a painful reminder of a "home front" at the face of war, fully four years after the 10 July 1940 start of the Battle of Britain. This murderous mayhem in which isolationist America stood by and watched the courageous Brits get bombed to oblivion, without lifting a finger. "Not our fight" they screamed, a half century before our 9/11 proves them wrong. It was a day of infamy for all living Americans of 1940.

Chapter Five - Part E
Hunting down a place with food in it!

Returning now back to 1944 Northwich, all modern conceptions of advertising are all shot to heck. We have to hunt down a place with food in it! We do find one small shop open. Glory be. A very small, hard to see sign out front reads: "Fish and Chips" in an arc at the top, and below that: "Tripe - Cowheels" and below that "Peas." Well, sorely we are hungry, but perhaps we should look elsewhere. Trapped by circumstance we stagger in with a bewildered yet hungry look on or faces. Ravenous, may be a better way to put it. Not unlike any long, narrow American drug and soda store, this dimly lit, secret little shop threatened to burst at the seams any minute.

It was jam packed with perhaps a full company of soldiers. Two elderly, rather well-endowed women dash madly about the store, their once jolly faces melted with fatigue. Yet their eyes were still aglow with the light of over anxiety and sincere desire to please the hapless crowd. Are these Brits great or what? This evening, thank the living Lord, they were serving chips and peas... period! (the Brit version of French fries). The peas tasted like soggy starch beat with a club, but the chips were hot and crispy, just drained of scalding grease. A darn nicely balanced meal I say... positively the best I have ever eaten!

One poor, bedraggled woman, more weary than the others, patiently alternately explained, pleaded, and argued out all the difficulties with the English monetary system! Close by a small young Brit, all of 4 years old, is hanging on to his dad's coat tails, near the end of the line. I look down quizzically: "What-cha got in your mouth, Sonny? As he looked up a huge grin stole over his tiny face, he hid his face in his dad's coattails and didn't say a word. Dad stood and beamed with pride, his eyes with a twinkle of intense, yet silent and observant interest. The same can be said of all Brits.

Chapter Five - Part F
"Pubs" or beer bars

We visit several other, of the countless "Pubs," or beer bars, placed here and there on every street. These are a cross between the USA "lodge clubhouse" and a classic saloon. Every night they are the "hangout" of choice for every living, breathing soul in town.

Here is one example. Through the inevitable gloomy doorway and down the equally dim hall we enter upon a scene bright with yelling, laughing, and singing the likes of which I have never seen before. They are definitely not like an American bar at all. There are several small rooms and a bar bubbling over with lousy beer and good wine. Other rooms are arranged like private parlors, some buzzing with the town gossip groups of old hens! Some with jolly old potbellied men! The strong aroma of beer and the haze of cigar smoke is everywhere, and a poker game jives in the corner.

In the side booth of a larger room sit six very old women like dignified statues, all guzzling beer! In another booth there was a loud cracking noise and an air of hostility as one old gentleman slapped the hand of another at the table. With some ferocity he snatches away a measly half pack of gum from a guy who was hogging it all. The pack of gum had been offered only moments ago by a well-intentioned GI. "I got kids too," he snaps and the hostility ceases!!!

Chapter Five - Part G
Departure by troop train down to Southampton embarkation

Dateline: **Saturday 7 Oct. 1944, Troop train southbound from Chester to Southampton**

With this inadequate glimpse of this old English countryside and Northwich we shall have to leave the whole of England. For at this very moment, I must finish this tale in France, on the eve of my entry into the thick of WW2. It has been a peaceful, rewarding interlude, never to be forgotten.

Dateline: **Sun. Oct. 8th. We take the train down to Southampton and Isle of Wight to board our landing ship bound for Omaha Beach.**

Today we are getting our gear in order, and it is substantial! Fully loaded up for the boarding formations I manage to hop on the scale and weigh myself. The needle swings around to well above the 200-pound mark. Ordinarily I weigh 143 lbs. so by subtraction we arrive at several conclusions. On the scale, I was carrying no duffle bag, just my rifle, belt, canteen, gas mask and pack. The guilty party seems to be the Mule-buster pack weighing 92 to 98 pounds. You know that a bag of cement weights SO many lbs. Try loading 2 of these on your back and then double timing at 5 miles per hour.

CHAPTER SIX
Replacement depot chain Normandy to Bayonne

Starting trek through Six Major Replacement Depot Chain

PREFACE REMARKS: The action timeline for this chapter covers the period 8 - 27 October 1944. The primary source documents are war letters written 63 years ago. WW2 is raging everywhere. It is 4 months after D-Day Normandy.

Chapter Six - Part A
Landing at Omaha Beach, D+129 Days, Troop transport ship crosses the channel
Small landing craft take us on into Omaha Beach. Perils of jumping 15ft. from shipside nets into gyrating LCI's.
Dateline: **Sunday 8 October 1944.**

Departing Southampton, harbor bound for the Normandy coast... We do so with a good deal less anxiety than the D-Day GI's of 6 June who were getting shot at. We do have our one big problem, but it is not life threatening, only a "pain-out" and obnoxious! It is at the usual early morning hour that we board our Troop Transport in Southampton harbor.

It is the infamous, 95 lb. Mule-buster pack, you learned about at the end of Chapter 5. This pack is aptly named. It measures about 26" wide x 32" high x 24" deep off one's back and weighs the equivalent of two sacks of cement. It sounds incredible, but there is a rational. This stems from the lack of a functional deep-water port anywhere along the north coast of France from Cherbourg to Antwerp. Hitler wrecked them all.

Most all students of WW2 know that the success of D-Day hinged on the fabulous Allied beaches along the coast from Omaha to Sword. The vital feature was the enormous, portable, modular, concrete caisson dock system. The British designed, built it in England, floated across the Channel and sunk off of Sword Beach. Good show, but one mighty storm gave this dock fits!!

Chapter Six - Part B
Lack of deep-water ports gives us the Mule-buster pack

The problem is that until the deep ports are cleared and operational (an enormous job, estimated not to be done until much later in war) the Brit dock at Normandy is overloaded, big time. You will also recall that one of the prime Hitler targets of the "Battle of the Bulge, North" in December was *again* the port of Antwerp. The Quartermaster Corps is having trouble just stocking (tons and tons of clothing, etc.) the vast array of Supply Depots behind all of the Western Fronts. This, to keep all Army Groups going. Enter the light-bulb idea: Use Replacement Troops as mules to carry the stuff over on their backs! This correspondent is just one of those thousands of mules! How we all coped or failed to cope with the task is at the heart of the story that unfolds below.

Arriving in England we had been carrying a standard pack and a huge duffle bag with a strap and a handle. This all changed at the Replacement Depot outside of Chester. In effect they dumped the entire duffle bag contents into the new Mule-buster packs, in extended mode.

This, on top of the Quartermaster underwear, and all the other legitimate gear already there. Two guys in my group have their packs rip under the strain. On marching breaks, we try to support the humongous dismounted pack, using the whole Rifle muzzle up as "tripod" leg. I wind up with three beautiful holes in the bottom of my pack where the muzzle has shoved clean through the tough canvas. Sitting down with the pack on is also disastrous. We maintain full control, slowly until we are about 18 inches from the ground. Then the final gap between body and ground is closed in an eyewink with a painful thud. With the pack on, the attempt to sit up is beyond the realm of physical possibility. We have to roll over on our stomach to gain sufficient leverage to get up. See what Hitler did by destroying all of our deep-water ports. What else can I say? Perils of the big jump... shipside net, into a bobbing LCI (Landing Craft Infantry); the saga of the Mule-buster packs. We contemplate all the above as we rock and roll across the English Channel in heavy seas. Several miles off the Omaha Beach we are met by an energetic and wildly bouncing LCI. The stage is set for a very sporty deal. We debark the big ship by monkey climbing down a huge, thick rope net hanging shipside off the starboard bow. It is something. Now hear this. The valiant GI's of D-Day did this without Mule-buster Packs, but some with the same equivalent weight in assault weapons, ammo and gear, etc.

All of this amidst the mayhem and thunderous barrage of 16-inch Battleship shells whooshing overhead.

Even under normal circumstances with light gear the jump from the bottom of this net, 8 to 18 ft. down into a bobbing LCI, already mostly full with GI's, can lead to broken legs, ankles on the jumper along with broken skulls and backs suffered by those he lands on!!! Now perhaps you are beginning to absorb the dimensions of the problem, whether or not you are getting shot at. Imagine, you are there... at the bottom of the net and have to make judgment calls that will affect your wellbeing and that of a bunch of GI's below.

Now Pilgrim, just to make things a tad sportier we have added two sacks of cement to your back. Is that 90 pounds comfy??? There are at least forty other guys above you trying to scramble down and get in the LCI. You take stock of what is below. Not only is the LCI heaving ten feet up and down relative to the big ship which is also rolling back and forth in the heavy seas... It is also moving 2 feet sideways in all directions. You cannot deliberate very long, but you have to aim and time your jump perfectly. If you wait until the LCI is down 10 feet (18-foot jump), disaster is absolutely certain.

A quick learner, you decide to jump as close as you can to when the jump is only 8 feet. You say your prayers, tighten the straps on your cement sacks, aim and jump! You accelerate at 32 ft per second per second on the way down and, by the grace of God, hit the small target only perhaps a shy yard square, with your knees bent just right, exactly between two other GI's... not on top of them. You collapse on top of your cement bags and give them a hug. You get a gold star, having accomplished mission impossible. You think most certainly you won't forget the experience... it is to remain locked in your brain for 63 years.

It is still locked in the brain of this correspondent... and you had better believe it. It happened for millions of GI's in both the European and Pacific Theaters. But you now shudder to realize you are only one for three on the way to the objective *dumping forever* your cement sacks.

Chapter Six - Part C
Debarking the LCI into the surf at Omaha. The big climb out up the bluff ramp and the pack dump

Close in to shore as possible the LCI bow ramp drops down and a whole platoon of cement sacks jumps out, thank the Lord, not getting shot at. We wade on in waist deep water doing our best to keep our gear dry. Now we are two for three.

Looming ahead in stark view is the long climb up the ramp on the side of the Omaha bluff. We had learned the hard way that navigating, even on flat land with the Mule-buster packs, it can be a real trial to keep one's balance and not stumble.

Gangways and long ramps are a whole new ballgame, especially with unseen obstructions on the trail. We knew stumbling meant winding up flat on your back and pack with one's feet sticking up uselessly in the air like a turtle. Self-recovery is impossible… help is required. So it is that we eye our objective. It is now only several hundred feet away at the top of the Bluff: The Quartermaster Drop Zone where we all can dump our Mule-buster packs forever, minus our standard military and personal equipment. We huff and puff up that hill with unmatched anticipation, and at the top… the roar of shouts and jumps for glee reverberate all across northern France.

We GI "Mules" have done our job and survived. All the military GI underwear and clothing accumulates by the ton in huge Quartermaster warehouse/tent, from there to be distributed by trucks all over the ETO.

Chapter Six – Part D
Hitler's Atlantic wall at D +130, …A vignette on the
status of the wall Gen. Rommel built
Dateline: **Tuesday 10 October 1944, in our Pup-Tent City, Vicinity Utah to Bayeux**
On and off we are free to explore the residuals from the D-Day mayhem throughout the Nazi fortifications. Hitler is already targeting his famous Gen. Rommel for failure and plots against him, and next Saturday, 14 October the mighty Irwin Rommel, hero of the Africa Corps will commit suicide. What a testimony to the ravages of the Nazi society of fear. Tomorrow, Wed. 10 Oct., US air raids start against Okinawa

This… is Normandy, France at D+130. Walking through the fortification ruins I see, firsthand, at least a segment of the overall pattern… invasion fortress Europe. In total, the residuals of what our exceedingly brave GI's were up against, and of the forbidding coastal terrain. There is a vast network of fortifications and chain tunnel foxholes the Germans soldiers learned to sleep in. It is from these they phoned back with some urgency to Nazi HQ at first daylight on 6 June: The entire sea is full of ships and Gummi-poopies (rubber dummies) are falling out of the sky.

Here and there is a lousy pill box with pretty, green grass growing out of the top. And I see what is left after our assault forces went through. A battered sign is swinging wildly in a stiff wind says, "off limits to all military personnel, mines not yet cleared." Close by a half-buried set of steps lead down into a dark, dank, moldy hole where they lived like rats. Dark and wet they are now filled with the trash of "C" Rations and here and there, some shredded German uniforms… now a bit soggy.

One pill box is a split mass of fractured concrete, a slab heaved up out of the earth with the torn ends of rebar sticking out all over the place. Enough light filters down there to reveal the tangled mass of an electrical switch board and nerve center. Conduits and heavy rubber power lines drape down over broken walls. In a word, just a hell of a mess!!!

Chapter Six – Part E
Replacement depot chain. Starts in Vicinity Bayeux to Rouen
Dateline: **Friday 13 Oct. - 15. 1944, Our pup-tent city, vicinity Utah to Bayeux**

The pouring rains have started, and all of us "W" guys, Wilkinson, Wests (two of us) and a Wes, etc. are all together close by in our corner of Pup-Tent City. Our gear is stored, and we are dry under taught stretched canvas, not known for spaciousness. Wes and I are together for now.

All told, Trevor Wilkinson (of the Mauretania) and I are together all across France to Luneville and Halloville. We must have been in the same tent at some point. I leave it up to his impeccable memory to reconstruct exactly where this was!

Chapter Six – Part F
Chow time in pup-tent city

The diet around here is the very latest in balance, variety and quantity. It is consistent in makeup and as savory, hot and steaming as ever passed the kitchen door of Grand Plaza Hotel in New York. For instance, yesterday morning we have Spam, nice and frosty, jam and dog biscuits. The latter item is conveniently cracked into edible portions with a heavy, steel trenching pipe.

At noon we have Spam, jam and dog biscuits, and in the evening, it is dog biscuits and Spam. Thirsty? Need something to wash the dog biscuits down? An adventurer, I slop 400 yards through the oozing mud to "The Kitchen." Glory be! I find there something from heaven… four huge, 50-gallon tubs bubbling over with Del Monte pineapple and grapefruit juice, just bubbling with cool foam on the surface. After it starts running out of my ears (a real bummer) I grab every container of any description I can find or swipe, fill them to overflow, and stagger back to Pup-Tent city. I share well and guess who is the hero of the day?

The Dog Biscuits, above, require some elaborative discussion. They are not really "Fido's Bone"… he could not handle them. They are daintily molded by 40-ton drop forge into the shape of a square block. We usually attack them with hard steel chisels!!

Chapter Six - Part G
The Hedgerow War of June and July... finally over

The infamous hedgerows of Normandy are huge four-foot-high ridge-mounds of earth with a jungle thick mass of vines, bushes and trees on top. They are not unlike those I saw near Chester, England, and they are the almost perfect concealment and cover for the defense. They border each and every road and farm field around here.

This hedgerow war of last June and July required the development of a whole new strategy and science of warfare, extremely risky for the offensive Army. One bright GI got an award for jury-rigging a massive, flat toothed weldment for the front of tanks, that, with enough kinetic energy and brute force could actually hit an eight-foot section of hedgerow, at 90 degrees, head on, and scoop it out of the way.

The problem is that a German 88 is usually zeroed in on the US tank as it breaks through. Veterans sent to the ETO from the Pacific say (according to the purple heart troops around here) they would rather face the whole dang, stifling hot, malaria infested jungle than to confront the hedgerows of Normandy. We owe a lot to our GI's who fought and finally broke through the hedgerows of Normandy.

Chapter Six - Part H
Amazing supply logistics (Truck and semi teams navigate
the mud and slop, getting supplies to the front)

Mud... thick, black, slippery mud is everywhere around here, supported by incessant rains. The other day I watched the great teamwork between the 2 ½ ton trucks and huge tractor trailers. Here it is man and machine against the mud. They line up three or four in a row, chained bumper to bumper, and after a howling approach they plow, growl and spit their way through the tougher parts. Terrific, sustained inertia and momentum is surely involved... not unlike the tough icebreakers of the Arctic Circle.

Chapter Six - Part I
Daily life in pup-tent city for the replacement soldier
Dateline: **Sunday 15 Oct. in our Pup-Tent City, Vicinity Utah to Bayeux**

There are a million guys gambling pinochle cards in our tent, so this correspondent is writing this letter from Ken West's tent. It takes some candlelight and persistence to stay up with Mail Call. It is still wetter than heck around here and I am having trouble with wet, soggy stamps and envelopes... they just don't work.

We are also getting a little perturbed wallowing around in the mud. Good news is that we are unlikely to stay here very long. A few days earlier, they make five entire replacement packets (Units) pack up their pup tents in the pitch dark, pouring rain and mud. Real fun and games.

This morning we find their entire field a total shamble. It is covered with forgotten equipment, carbines, belts, packs, gas masks, etc. Under the circumstances, could we expect much more? I surely hope so from this correspondent soldier. The management of a complex assortment of both combat and personal gear, on the fly under the worst conditions, is key to staying alive in the face of war. There is more coming on this subject as all of this gear is consolidated or pitched along long hike to Luneville. The longer a marginal item is carried, the more likely it is that it will get pitched.

Here you have two guys horsing around in a very confined space and head room trying their best to keep from freezing, stow all of their gear and get some vital sack time. It isn't easy. Many readers have tried this on campouts in peacetime. At the stark face of war, it is an entirely different ballgame. The pup-tents are made out of GI shelter halves, snapped together.

The GI Army blankets are OK, and extras are available from Unit Supply, but the huge, 3-inch blanket safety pins are missing. This requires the home front to pitch in. Without them there is no way to keep toes, feet, legs & arms from sticking out.

There are a thousand things on the mind of each soldier in this camp: apprehensions and worries of all sorts. Each is left to ponder his own fate. This correspondent is clearly an "operator," and incredibly he is interested in having the home front supply chain dispatch a favorite protractor-ruler. Says he wants to work out some angles on this situation. Who is to argue? He then goes back to reading the Army magazine, "Yank" by candlelight. This is the face of war.

Chapter Six - Part J
Replacement depot chain continues through vicinity Reims

Night of Tuesday 17 October - The consolidation of equipment continues. Sure enough, it is a cold and rainy night that the "W" section of Pup-Tent City is rousted out for the move. We board a long string of Army 2 ½ ton trucks for the long, tortuous route west and south behind the ''Western Front. Wisely we are not routed through Paris, liberated 25 August... it is a transport nightmare.

We arrive at our new Replacement Depot Wednesday 18 October, to be our last Depot in tents. Gradually we are getting our gear waterproofed, consolidated & compacted. It is a long, soul searching process. Mail Call logistics continue to be a problem with wet stationary, envelopes and stamps. Waterproofing these packets and maintaining our supply of wax candles is a high priority. We are waiting to be assigned to a specific, combat Infantry Division.

Chapter Six - Part K
Depot chain continues south to Neufchâteau
Dateline: **21 Oct.- "Civilized" now in vicinity Nancy:**

On the truck ride down here, we go through a myriad of towns in a major French Wine District (All censored in WW2). Finally, we're getting civilized, out of the tents into permanent stucco houses which the Krauts forgot to burn down... or they didn't have time. Gone too are the infamous dog biscuits above. They are replaced by GI "K" and "C" rations, loaded with yummy, very high density, dark chocolate bars and fruit bars, along with canned delights and powdered drinks of all types.

Chapter Six - Part L
Sunday church services on logs, sawdust & chips

Mail Call logistics continue in the dead of night. Up here in our quaint, cozy "Hay Loft" this correspondent is perched on top of four "C" ration crates as both bench and writing table. Wow… are we civilized or what? The soft light of a neat, snitched light bulb illuminates the cheery scene, replacing wax candles, for now.

The morning church services are something else... we really get a lot out of them. Confoundedly, as testimony to how recently the Germans had departed the end of the building hall (our church) is plastered with big, black, lousy, obnoxious NAZI Eagle-Swastika. German National Emblem, still in place after four long years under the Nazi jack boot. The building is a huge armory with a sawdust and wood chip floor. Big logs are thrown on the floor to provide seating…"war zone," lowbrow pews. But it is a church, with everyone there for the same purpose. They even have a little "ersatz" (make-do) organ, blowing its lungs out for the troops. The Army Chaplains do a great job, the first of many as the face of war rages through Lorraine and Alsace.

This is about the third major Replacement Depot (skipping the Tent Cities) we have been in since we hit Omaha beach. Captured and recaptured many times by the Krauts, the French and the Americans, it is a regular, French built Army garrison. It is a huge, stone stucco barracks, topped with a red tile roof and at least a dozen chimneys.

It is four times larger than the typical American barracks in the States. Our home here sure beats the foxholes in our future. We are situated up in a long, storage attic, dark as heck, but with dry floors a big bunch better than the typical pup-tent site. Electric and water facilities are lousy, but the chow is darn good… typically foreign.

The whole place is surrounded by a huge wall, making it difficult to get "illegal" passes. The pouring rains continue, and I still marvel at how the supply trucks plow through it. The jeeps around here are like the energizer bunny… they just keep going and going. But shades of the impossible, the other day I witness one actually stuck in the mud!

Chapter Six – Part M
French kids and their interpreters

It is in the year 1942, as a sophomore at Westfield, New Jersey High School that this correspondent learns the rudiments of the German language from Mr. Shaterian, our irrepressible teacher-mentor. Affectionately we call him "Shadrack," and he teaches us by learning German poems, stories and fables and reciting them at academic contests all over the State.

At the time I simply didn't have a clue of how valuable an asset this was to be…or of the void in my life that would be created by my failure to take French as well. So here we are, perhaps near Nancy, France in 1944. French kids abound everywhere, and they are motor-mouth, non-stop talkers. For those of us that don't parley French the communications block is devastating, and we are very much in debt to our French speaking fellow GI's. They are our interpreters and they save the day. The kids are profoundly grateful to every single American GI for their liberation from the Nazi jackboot and have insatiable curiosity.

Little French kids in their berets, shorts, and black bunting jackets trot all around this Garrison. Most are 8-10 years old, they bum cigarettes for Papa and chocolate, etc. for themselves from American soldiers. Such is the nicotine addiction grip on European society that cigarettes are the de-facto currency of choice.

Papa may just use them for money. This correspondent is a non-smoker, but I get a packet of three in each K-Ration box which I then trade or give away. This evening I come upon a huddle of GI's around two little Kids… all eyes fixed with total dependence upon the soldier acting as interpreter. I am fascinated by the long string of perfect, high speed French lingo from these little guys. The star French kids, 8-14 years old, captivate the GI Audience. One of them with the cutest baby face and sparkling eyes claims he is 14 years old, yet not an inch over 3'1" tall with a normal build. He just can't be over 8 years. We all groan with disbelief. He insists he will bring back his birth certificate to prove his age. I think he was just starved for 4 years by the Nazis.

Most of the kids haven't seen a sliver of chocolate since 1940. All have been doing without for so long that they prefer to barter for cigarettes and actual goods as opposed to French francs, currently exchanged at 50 francs to the dollar. The kid claims that several of his friends had nearly died from poison candy given to them by a German/Nazi soldier in 1942.

All of this is verified by a French doctor; 8 or 14 years old, whatever... this kid is certainly articulate. The US Medical Corps has done much for the local population since D-Day.

The star kid loves ice-cream (astonishing). He knows what it is but only remembers tasting it once. With a little persuasion we get all the kids to sing "La Marseillaise". However, this is only after two of them have a long serious debate over who is going to sing and who is going to break the ice with the first line. As the clinching incentive we give them each a couple of bars of official US Army, "D" ration, dark chocolate bars and they start singing like mad!

What a duet! Oh bummer, for the lack of a 2007 camcorder. So, we bid adieu to this captivating, peaceful interlude from the raging face of war. On the whole it seems that the French haul of cigarettes, gum and chocolate from the GI is substantial.

Chapter Six – Part N
Our final replacement depot and assignment to the 79th Division
Dateline: **Friday 27 October -** *Orphans no more* **... we belong to a Combat Outfit.**
The New York Times of 22 November reports that the Big Blue 79 (the 79th Infantry Division) is in action with General Patche's 7th Army east of Nancy. In the course of the next month we are sure to find this out. For now, this Friday in October, I sit, catching up on mail call in a Special Service Tent.

This is in an Advanced Replacement Depot just east of Nancy, France... the eastern threshold of the Province Lorraine. Power lines sport real electric lights and a modern, short wave Radio Set purring away in the corner, GI's crowded all around. There are extensive American Expeditionary Forces radio broadcast facilities in Europe. The broadcasts are coming in via a magnificent short wave, national hook-up from the States. Included are Voice of America commentators and other broadcasting stations. Familiar programs such as Fulton Lewis Jr., Amos and Andy, Inner Sanctum, and all the rest.

Shades of all it means to be home... for the teenage soldiers of 1944. This, along with the American Forces Newspapers: "Stars and Stripes" and "Yank," are doing a darn good job to keep us abreast of the news, at least until we get into the thick of combat. Then, this correspondent is totally in the dark...with the Battle of the Bulge, North, for instance.

We are back in Pup-Tents again temporarily, but becoming remarkably efficient in this sort of life, rolling up blankets and bedrolls in record time to "nothing flat" We have packed and unpacked our still very big, "transport" packs (as opposed to combat packs) so many times that we now use only a 2-ton pile driver to ram the stuff in.

My new address is now: Pvt. Harrison West 42018762 (my Army serial number that still resides in my brain after 63 years) Company B, 315th Infantry, APO 79, c/o Postmaster, New York, New York. It means a heck of a lot to a guy not to be kicked around like an orphan anymore.

In Chapter 7 to follow, we will be ensconced in the Bayonne Rest & Training Area, just south of Luneville, France, and pick up the story from there. The honeymoon is over. Things are about to change and our touristy, sight-seeing days are history. This correspondent shoots off a barrel of pride in the Big Blue 79, the world's greatest combat fighting force. The "old-timers" I join here have been on the line ever since D Day, continually for about 150 days without rest. They have earned the name.

CHAPTER SEVEN

Bayonne rest area... south of Nancy and Luneville, France Home of the Fighting 7th COMBAT INF. DIVISION

PREFACE REMARKS: The action timeline for this chapter covers the period 28 Oct. to 9 Nov. 1944. The primary source documents are war letters written 63 years ago. WW2 is raging everywhere. It is 5 months after D-Day Normandy.

Chapter Seven - Part A
The ninth hour; prelude to combat.
Dateline: **Saturday 28 Oct. 1944 - The cobblestone Streets of Bayonne, France**

These are peach fuzz lads of every description, 30 in all, gangling GI's that were recently but names on a list at Division Replacement Headquarters. Tiny patches of French kids gawk, a wobbly old cart creaks off down along the side of the road, a dog barks, and a few old women pause briefly in the doorways. This Platoon of slung M-1 rifles (brand new ones) and oversized packs ambles through the cobblestone streets of this rustic town of Bayonne, France. Shortly they push through the gates into the courtyard of an old schoolhouse. Inside, the First Platoon of Baker Company was being snapped around the yard by an ordinary looking drill (Sgt.).

These boys have seen action and combat, but it is still a mystery to us. They sure could spot us "a mile away" as we moved in through the gates like chicks just broken from the shell. Here are a bunch of clean faces, new clothes, ridiculously "mulish" packs, and half with the shipping numbers still scrawled across the front of our helmets. This is to be our combat outfit, Baker Company, 315th Infantry Regiment of the Big Blue 79. We watch the "old men" (all of 20-26) half expecting them to be different or something. They watch us in *horror* (not really) and are glad to see us... long needed help to replace their dead and wounded buddies.

Our smooth-talking Platoon Sergeant gives us the general idea of what the score is. Red headed Lt. Ryan, Co Exec Officer, pauses as he comes out of the orderly room and talks to us a few impromptu minutes. He and Nixon (along with our Squad Sergeant Gerry Cone, below) really impress me. Incredibly, I am to meet them half a century later at 1996-98 reunions of the 315th Regiment in Lexington and Columbus, before they all pass away. Lt. Ryan says me and the boys are in a business with a job to do. We are joining them in that business. His posture is to accept all courses events may take, making the best of what they had, and taking orders as they came. We all have a war to win.

So again, what does the Infantry Dogface (of the Mauldin, Willy and Joe cartoons) have to look forward to? The good news is that there is no "Tour of Duty" in the Infantry, as in the Air Force. The bad news is he joins the "March of Time." For him this means that ominous, resounding tramp-tramp-tramp, yard by yard, second by second towards that "Ninth Hour" at which he is either killed, wounded or captured. There's no other escape. This is both reality & the price we pay for our freedom today!

The millions of Dogfaces of WW2 in both Europe (ETO) and the Pacific (CBI) face this reality each and every day with incredible courage and purpose of mind. In the ETO (European Theater of Operations) war, it is necessary to drive/pound/push the Infantry Divisions incessantly for 125 to 150 continuous days on the line without a rest break.

This might be 2-3 huge island campaigns in the CBI. The Infantry and Marine war doesn't stop for anybody. If a GI lets this "March of Time" dominate his every train of thought, he will break in no time at all. Americans today can thank the Lord that the vast majority of Dog Faces push these thoughts way back to the rear burner and move on! This is what keeps America free!!!

Contrary to what we expect, the experienced, old-timers rarely go off into sprees telling us what combat was like D-Day through October. It would have been counterproductive for both parties. We glean it by innuendo. It is difficult to give a graphic picture of our Company strength, losses and replacements.

Prior to coming offline, the normal typical squad, full strength of 12 had been cut down to 8 over a month of fighting. We replacements bring it back up to full strength. For seven days we all are put through a rigorous training and conditioning regime, needed by all newcomers!

Productively, during this period Platoons and Squads are reorganized with specific job designations for each guy. New clothing and equipment are issued. The main item of new, winterized equipment is the "shoe-pack"... an Army version of the LL Bean hunting boot with leather hi-tops and rubber bottoms.

Issued from one to two sizes too large to allow space for extra heavy insoles and socks. Good in theory, but they later turn out to be a disaster. Bed rolls are made up of two blankets as a sleeping bag and shelter halves to be carried by the Company Jeeps.

Chapter Seven - Part B
Hello God - at the Face of War.
Dateline: Sun. 29 October 1944 - A Prayer on the eve of combat

Of all of the complex influences at work on the souls of the American GI of any faith, in WW2 none surpass that of almighty God, our supreme creator. The embodiment of the 1944 Chaplain Corps of the US Army is, of course, fully multi-denominational. It covers the core beliefs of our Founding Fathers of 1776-1789, overwhelmingly Christian. It also acknowledges our basic Judeo-Christian heritage. All services cover our Catholic, Protestant and Jewish soldiers. The issues presented by soldiers who claim to be an atheist present an entirely different problem. In the 21st Century through 2007, there has been a disturbing campaign by the Atheist ACLU (a de-facto arm of one of our two political parties in the USA) to kick God out of the United States of America.

Without going off on a 10-page tangent, let this soldier correspondent make it abundantly clear: There is no way in blazes the ACLU has ever been able to, or ever will be able to kick God out of the life of the Dog Face, American GI. We can all thank the Lord for this. Excerpts follow.

Pass this acid test, and indeed you are a bonified, registered atheist. "Arrange for this shell burst totally to shred the helmet liner, without killing you, just drawing a little skull blood. Further, in the subsequent milliseconds, arrange to have your body hit the ground with a jarring thud, bloody but still alive, wondering just what in the hell happened, and all of *this... without uttering the name of your maker*".

If the words "Dear God... God, Almighty" or the like' come out of your mouth... you are not an atheist. Get real and join humanity. A couple of combat vets from the Big Blue 79 have arranged the basic components of the above acid test.

To the above preface remarks I call the reader's attention to four, remarkable prayers and pieces of WW2:

"His Signal Answered" a prayer by sailor Billy Hicks

"Up or Down...Which Way you Went" an inscription on a tombstone

"Censored" by Navy Radioman, Harbeck

The Seaman's Version of the 23 Psalm

To all of these I add the following prayer, authored by a soldier on the eve of combat, framed in the mold of a naive young atheist kid, struggling with his previous ideas about life and religion:

"Hello, God" -soldier author, unknown young naive atheist, just beginning to think. (edited 2007, H. West)

Look, God... I have never spoken to You,

But now I want to say..."How do you do?"

You see, God, they told me you didn't exist

And, like a fool, I believed all of this.

Last night from a shell hole I saw your sky,

I figured right then, they had told me a lie,

Had I taken the time to see the things you made

I'd have known they weren't calling a spade a spade

I wonder, God, if you'd shake my hand,

Somehow, I feel that you will understand.

Funny, I had to come to this hellish place,

Before I could see your shining face.

Well, I guess there isn't much more to say,

But I'm sure glad, God, I met You today,

I guess the zero hour will soon be here,

But I'm not afraid since I know you are near.

The signal! Well, God, I'll have to go,

I like you lots, this I want you to know,

Look now, this will be a horrible fight,

Yet I know, with Your help, I'll end all right.

Though I haven't known you much before,

I wonder, God, if you'd wait at your door,

Look now, I'm crying! Me! Shedding tears,

I wish I'd known you all of these years.

Well, I have to go now, God, adieu-

Strange how much stronger I feel, knowing you

Countless books on WW2 skirt this issue. "Sunshine Soldier" shall not. This issue is at the heart and soul of the Price of Freedom, the single most misunderstood and ignored factor in the 21st Century. We are at a crossroads, when again we find the United States of America fighting for the survival of civilization.

It is in a world when half of the USA and most of the rest of the world refuses to acknowledge any threat or confront any evil. Why? Aside from the total absence of courage and vision, Heaven forbid, "People might get killed." This is a prevailing theme that totally ignores the reality consequence of toothless inaction. In the era of rampantly available nuclear bombs it is absolutely guaranteed to lead to millions and millions more people getting killed (incinerated). Not just the several thousand currently being killed in the freedom confrontations of 2007.

Now enter again… God and war. The only way to confront this issue in 1944 and today is head-on.

Chapter Seven - Part C
My words to my parents on the eve of the Allied push into Lorraine
Dateline: **5 November 1944 - The Rest and Training Area in Bayonne/Luneville, France**
"Well Mom and Dad, it seems we have a little problem to work on together. It is the same situation millions of other families have faced and are facing in the firm, comforting hand of God, in years gone by, ever since 1776. In this war people all around us have brothers, sisters and sons in harm's way on fighting fronts all over this world.

These people really place a very high value on their freedom and have a vital stake in this world conflict. I sort of figure if it is good enough for them, it is good enough for us. I have never known anyone whose mind is in such close harmony with God as is yours. Believe me, I have come to realize the infinite power of God,

With this realization I know I shall be able to face this situation or any future situation on the road of life. I write this letter almost coincident with my first combat action in Lorraine. From now on for the duration of this combat status will be a matter of course, on and off, fighting and resting. I believe in the job we are doing and that it must be done. So, do you, and in their gut, so do all Americans today

When this mess is over, Mom and Dad, I am coming home. This I know… this you must know as well… we cannot know or think anything else. Gee, but it is nice to know that through all of this cold, dank, mist and mud that is today, there looms a tomorrow so bright it cannot be fully conceived.

Entirely aside from this, God has given us so many other reasons to be thankful for. Let's just say I am lucky for want a better way to put it. I am lucky that I was not among those boys in Bataan, who fought with their bare hands and courage against hopeless odds... the same for the boys of Wake Island, Dunkirk, and a long list of the dark days of WW2... the darkest hours ever, before dawn. Those boys fought a losing War yet did not ever even think of cutting and running.

The very same can be said for the dark days of 1776. This is what is takes to keep going when freedom is threatened. This why America is free, and we can thank God for it.

I am also lucky, Mom and Dad that I am fighting as a part of unit that is in turn part of a mass of organized force. It is a dynamic force without equal...four, full Allied Armies, the Americans together with the Brits, Canadians, and French. I am moving with the winning side, with better and more equipment.

I am also lucky, Mom and Dad, because as a replacement I hit my Big Blue 79 outfit and had a couple of weeks to get settled and to know the guys before seeing action. This means a lot, you know. The current chances are nine to one that a typical replacement will go right up to the front lines after he hits France and get acquainted with his unit under fire.

So, Mom and Dad, you see we have just another situation of face, a lot to be thankful for, and everything to look forward to. Our biggest problem will be Mail Call communication time lag. I will know exactly when I am threatened during attacks and when I am safe. Like all Moms, all over the USA at any given moment, you and Dad simply will not know whether I am dead or alive.

This is a tough burden to bear. It will require both faith and prayers to handle it. I know you guys will do well. There will be times when I am busier than usual and/or run out of foxhole candles but will write at every possible moment I get. Well, Mom and Dad, keep that old gas stove cooking... I love you all, Harrison."

Chapter Seven - Part D
The Cross of Lorraine - The Big Blue 79 Patch
Dateline: 1 Nov.1944 - 79th Inf. Div. at rest, after 132 days on the line

The Cross of Lorraine means a lot to all of France, and to Lorraine in particular. It is an ornate cross with two crossbars at the top, one shorter, and below that a longer one, forming a "triangle" topped cross. It was the symbol of Joan of Arc, and under this banner she led her crusade for freedom… a very famous era in French History.

Under this banner the 79th Infantry Division (the Big Blue 79) sailed for home from France after initiating the first breakout through the Hindenburg line. This event led directly to the defeat of Germany in WW1 of 1918. After D-Day of WW2 in 1944 the 79th Division was officially credited with the capture of the Port of Cherbourg, first to cross the Seine River, and first to enter Belgium.

The Cross of Lorraine was awarded by the French to the 79th as its official insignia at the end of WW1. The 79th shoulder patch is an elegant shield of brilliant blue, with a bordered Cross of Lorraine in the middle - silver or white. Gen. De Gaulle has adopted the symbol for his staff. In WW2 and today, for all French and particularly for the people of Lorraine, it always brings up high levels of emotional response.

The Cross the Big Blue 79 and the price of freedom!
Dateline: June 1996 - an American retrace of the 1944 Liberation Battle Route!

On our West family return trip along the Lorraine Liberation Battle Route, this same blue Cross of Lorraine patch elicits an equally emotional, counter response by our whole family of 8 adults. This is something else. We have just departed our Luneville Hotel for the parking lot. We are gathered around our two minivans when a few of the local's spot that shiny Cross of Lorraine on the tall crown of my white bill cap. The reaction is electric. Instantly they also recognize that this is the patch of the Big Blue 79, a prime Division that had liberated Luneville in 1944. Excited words pass quickly, back and forth.

Within a scant minute this small group of humanity, Americans and French alike, are bawling together, out of control, amidst the sunny crisp air in this parking lot. Half of America, listen up. This is for real. These people know what it is like to lose one's freedom. They place a very high value on their freedom and those valiant men who gave it back to them!

Chapter Seven - Part E
Stateside background of the Big Blue 79 in WW2, 1942

The reactivated 79th Division starts out at Camp Pickett, Virginia. They follow on to Camp Blanding, Florida… then to Tennessee maneuvers… and to Camp Laguna Arizona. Coming back east they are at Camp Phillips, Kansas for a spell during the turn of the year 1943-44.

Finally, through the Boston POE, they ship overseas to join the mighty D-Day invasion troops. In their overseas record through October 1944, they have never failed to accomplish their mission or to take the designated objective. Gen. George Patton personally ranks the 79th as the fourth best of the myriad of US Infantry Divisions! Switched back and forth after D-Day, they endure 132 straight days of combat without relief. This is the longest period endured by any Div. to date.

Chapter Seven - Part F
Daily life in and out of the Bayonne HQ barracks
Dateline: 1 November 1944 - The Big Blue 79… at rest, after 132 days on the line

This place is right on the ball, a far cry from the Pup-Tent "camp outs" in the mud. We take time out to make visits to cities all around us, from Le Mans to Orleans and Neufchateau. We are getting a tad cold at night, so the "boys' go out on a recon mission and bring back as stove for our "living room"… nice and cozy heat!

The beds are built something like those real long, sloped shelf beds at Fort Niagara, NY. On those the soldiers slept side by side, the shortest at one end and the longest at the other! In the middle of the night the Sergeant would bellow out the command "Flip," and the whole bunch would flip over on their other sides. In the morning he bellows out "Fall Out," and all the guys literally fell out of bed! Now you know where the term came from. I kid you not.

Here, back home at the ranch in Bayonne, the "shelf" is on the floor. There is no slant and there is no short and long end. There is, however, a lot of straw and much more room. We eat very well, but seconds don't fill me up. We see movies every night! For relaxation we take "lollygag and letter writing" boat rides on the local canals.

Tough life. We have a hard time getting Big Blue 79, Cross of Lorraine shoulder patches around here. Every shipment that comes in gets appropriated and worn by the local population! Every gal in town proudly wears one. For the GI's the shortage is for real. The new 79th replacements have to use pen and ink to mark the Cross of Lorraine patch image on their combat jackets. We get passes into Luneville frequently, where again, the angel American Red Cross gals manage the coffee and donut lines to the delight of all GIs.

Chapter Seven – Part G
Special Services Div. (ASD) boosts GI morale
Dateline: **6 Nov.1944 - In Luneville, Army ASD and American Red Cross**

We often get town passes into Luneville, just a few miles north of Bayonne. Here the US Army Special Services Division (ASD) and the American Red Cross, all over the ETO are doing a fantastic job of raising the morale of the US Troops, this correspondent included. The ASD are the guys that provide top line motion pictures and live shows (Bob Hope and the like) in the most remote locations close to the front.

Nobody, no how, knows what a great morale booster it is to see an American made film in France, along with the USO in the States! But here in Luneville, seeing a show from the States, it really hits our home... away from home, like a ton of bricks. It is like living for 100 minutes in another world, completely oblivious of physical location and in the midst of a war raging close by.

The ASD runs a 16mm film per Battalion per evening, with nine Battalions in the Big Blue 79. These are mostly class A and B musicals and comedies produced within the last two years, but with good horse sense, they include absolutely no war pictures. The selection of titles is fantastic. We have been lucky that films we had missed seeing in the States, assumed lost forever, we have seen here in Bayonne or Luneville.

Chapter Seven – Part H
American Red Cross gal volunteer units

A word or two about these noble gals 1944-45. In all of France there are ten "Food and Entertainment Units." Each unit has 32 girls, 7 mobile donut and coffee kitchens, and one "Cinemobile" show truck. This amazing truck includes a couple of songbirds and an "8 to the bar," Boogie Woogie Theater.

The girls are beautiful beyond belief, talk smoothly and sensibly rather than small talk jabbering. They are all decked out navy blue ski suits with sharp looking paratrooper combat boots. The food trucks are virtual "Donut Dynamos," grinding out incredible quantities in no time at all. Compared to the Infantry dog face troops these gals live like queens.

Eventually I am to encounter one of the best of them, all in a mind-blowing experience. They have given up a high level of life in the States for this job, supporting the troops in the ETO. They could have kept it all at the drop of a finger by just saying no, but they didn't. This clearly separates them from half of 2007 America who have not one clue about what "support the troops" really means.

CHAPTER EIGHT

7th army push off to liberate Lorraine through to the Saverne Gap.

Combat action on the Lorraine-Alsace liberation battle route. On the line with the 315th Inf. from Montigny to Reipertswiller, Alsace

PREFACE REMARKS: The action timeline for this chapter covers the period 10 November 10 - 23 1944. The primary source documents are war letters written 63 years ago. WW2 is raging everywhere. It is 5 months after D-Day Normandy.

Dateline: **Friday to Monday 10-13 Nov.1944**

At the end of the ninth hour prelude to combat we replacement guys all feel a strange remoteness, not yet knowing what it means to be scared. With advanced packing and preparation Friday and Saturday, the move out order comes down.

We pile on 2 ½ ton trucks after dark Saturday evening for the 11-mile ride to the North East. We arrive at Foret de Mondon at 0200 hours in total Sunday darkness, bivouacking for the night. Inevitably the weather is cold, wet and rainy for the three battalions of the 315th Reg.

The Sunday attack plan calls for Canon Company to precede all the Rifle Companies. The attack is to be led by the 3rd Battalion, followed by the 2nd Battalion, with the 1st Battalion to follow in reserve.

Our objective is Montigny. This correspondent is in the 2nd Platoon of B Company, in the reserve. Monday morning, we all have a fit getting all of our gear together, in the dark. I do OK, but succeed in losing my personal, small utility knife. It is normally strapped to my boot top but is now lost somewhere in the soggy mud. Bummer.

Chapter Eight - Part A
The sad saga of the German tank & our friendly fire KIA
Dateline: Monday 13 November 1944 - the 9-mile trek to Reherrey

The tale of this sad saga is in living color in the DVD, "What Price- Freedom?" (501) 5.4 hours, taped in 2002, by the 26 vets/family at the 315th Reunion, in Milwaukee.

In the wee dark hours of Monday morning we move out with the rest of the 1st Battalion on the 6-mile trek east in the direction of Reherrey. The entire 1st Battalion, in a very long, single file line is marching through the very dense forest (Foret de Mondon), Rifles are slung and locked. The plan had been to use our 1st Battalion in a reserve role, to be committed only if necessary, and to clean up any pockets of resistance the other two had to bypass.

In reality, the 2nd & 3rd Battalions are about 3 hours ahead of us in a side by side attack mode. They are to arrive at Reherrey at 0630, cross the Verdurette River, attack and clear Montigny of Germans by 1000 hours, without any help from us. For the most part, this puts us in the role of soldier tourists. It would seem that all we have to do is to witness the mayhem the 2nd and 3rd Battalions have created on the trail, get ourselves to Reherrey, and then… cross the river and find our billets in Montigny. It doesn't work out that way... not by a long shot.

About three miles out it is our Baker Company's turn to file past a devastating scene. This correspondent is up front of the 2nd Squad (in the 2nd Platoon) near Harry Ballentine and Gerry Cone Squad Leader. Pete and Mexico, our inseparable team, bring up the rear. On our left there appears to be a classic scene from a Hollywood movie ... but it is not... it is for real.

A German tank knocked out several hours ago is still hot and smoldering. The entire German crew is seemingly dead or half dead, hanging out of the turret and sprawled all over the ground, every which way to Sunday. The long column draws a big deep breath and keeps plodding on. Up front in our squad none of us note any particular motion or threat of any kind.

In the rear, Mexico has a sharper eye. Out of the corner of his eye he witnesses one of the half dead Krauts propping himself up on his left elbow, wildly swinging a potato MASHer (a German hand grenade on a short stick handle) with his right arm. He is seconds away from throwing the damn thing at the column of GI's.

By pure reflex, seemingly in milliseconds, Mexico on-slings his rifle, unlocks it, and pumps a couple of rounds into the would-be killer, ensuring his permanent demise. End of story?? Not quite. Un-noticed by any of us, Mexico forgets to re-lock his rifle! The stage is set for total disaster... a terrible tragedy, at the face of war!

The column plods on without further event. In another few miles we find ourselves on the eastern bank of the Verdurette River just south of Reherrey aghast at what we see and wondering how the 2nd & 3rd Battalions attack Montigny, cross that river and remain in fighting condition. At the time we arrive all of the bridges have been blown.

Normally a small, dinky rural stream, it is now a raging torrent at least 10 yards wide. An image of West VA white water. But they got across before the bridges were blown. In any event, we have no recourse but to ford the raging water in all of our gear and dressed heavy, long, woolen overcoats.

These overcoats weigh a ton dry. They double that when wet. No time to twiddle thumbs and agonize. The whole dang column fords the river and now it is our turn. Viewing the scene from the western bank, we all take stock. On the far, eastern bank, Sgt. McGruder (not his real name) of another platoon, is helping pull the guys out of the torrent.

The really tall guys go across holding their rifles above their heads and make it up the far bank with some difficulty. Medium height guys like this correspondent, 5'11" at the time, find the water up to their chest and have a major problem maintaining a footing in the sheer force of the current.

I have the misfortune to witness the following event firsthand from the western bank... to burn in my memory forever. Comes time for little Mexico to venture into this torrent. Immediately be finds the water at neck level, and is struggling just to breathe, while staying vertical with full field pack, gear and the rifle above his head.

Sgt. McGruder on the eastern bank is pulling guy after guy up and out by grabbing on to the muzzle of each guy's, outstretched rifle. He does so with a mighty yank of the ton of wet, soggy soldier, overcoat and gear. He also does this with the muzzle of each rifle held inches from his own heart and vectored dead center on it.

Now comes little Mexico, He is gasping for air and struggling for his life itself, with a death grip on the trigger of his rifle. At this point on the whole 315th audience watching this saga unfold gives one huge groan anticipating the inevitability of what is to happen next, and with that totally helpless feeling.

Sgt. McGruder's favorite expression was. "Oh, you Dopey Hick!" The God-awful loud crack pierces our ears the instant the shot rings out. My recollection is that the Sergeant gets halfway through the word "Dopey" and that is it. His totally relaxed body slithers down into that raging stream, his two, cork-like-legs floating lazily in the cold grassy marsh, his arms spread out as if to say, "What is the use?"

We all agonize the "what-ifs."

What if - that German tank soldier had just died without trying to throw that grenade?

What if - Mexico had just locked his rifle after he shot the threatening Nazi soldier?

What if - The German charge to blow the bridge had mis-fired? Etc. Etc. Etc.

Reality is: For safety purposes it's totally impractical for GI's to keep locking and unlocking their rifles during the course of an on-going battle. "Friendly Fire" casualties always seem to surface at the face of all wars. This is just one of the life-changing events I encounter in WW2. Perhaps some readers might be able to live through an incident like this and then forget it. This soldier correspondent cannot. It won't go away!! Such was the gripping impact upon me in 1944 that I put the entire into saga into a poem. Mostly free verse, it still needs a lot of work, but is OK enough for the time being.

Chapter Eight - Part B
A soldier's poem at first combat
Dateline: **11-13 Nov. 1944, Luneville, Foret de Mondon to Liberation of Montigny, France**
Pfc. H. West, 2nd Squad, 2nd Platoon, Baker Co., 315th Inf., 79th Division, XV Corps.

[Note: This poem still needs work, *but it is virtually unchanged* since I wrote it 58 years ago. A life altering moment for me, this sad image of a "friendly fire" KIA is burned in my brain forever. It was my *very first,* eyewitness, combat KIA of WW2, crossing the swollen Verdurette River, just west of Montigny. H. West, 4 April 2003]

To trudge through the rain and mud in a sloppy chill of Fall,

Bent to the blasting wind that stings and cuts relentlessly through

To turn back the blinding storm with a half-shut eye,

To keep on moving...To say "I must."

That fella up ahead there... He's just a kid, and he keeps going… and I will too!

That fella behind me... He mumbles the same words and follows through.

To trudge through the rain and mud in a sloppy chill of Fall,

And say "Dear God… Thanks"

Thanks, Dear God… you see I'm moving and so I am warm

"My feet are aching... that blister stings…

"My right foot is throbbing... It hurts a whole mess

"But there will come a time when I can rest, and for that time,

I'd like to thank you, Dear God."

To flip and flop through a stream swollen by rain,

With the ice-cold water gushing to the depths of my boots,

And starting to seep through the bottom like the pressure of combat pain,

To hold a miserable piece of wood and steel high above your head,

 and say, "Dear God... thanks,"

This water is cold... it's over my head.

The current is swift... I am soaked to the skin and bone.

"But I'm almost across to the other bank,

And when I'm there... well, maybe not then,

But perhaps tonight, if we take this town,

I'll have a cozy warm stove to get dry again,

And so Dear God, - "Thanks for that time."

That fella there on the far bank, a great Sergeant ever more.

A soldering guy and a good Joe too,

I remember once when I was real hungry and had nothing,

He gave me a whole K-ration... He didn't have to... it was his loss

He always used to say: "Oh... you Dopey Hick!"

Now his mouth is open... I think he got halfway through the "Dopey"

His eyes are open too... in a lousy, glassy stare at the gathering mist above

His two "cork-like legs" floated lazily in the grassy marsh,

Flat on his back... his arms spread out as if to say. "What is the use!"

He was just trying to help other fellas get across the stream

But that little Mexican GI forgot to lock his gun,

The sharp, single crack of "Mexico's" rifle pierced our ears.

Hit the Sergeant straight through the heart... and then it was all done!

Chapter Eight - Part C
The big dry out by the cozy hot stoves of Montigny

It is a miserable, cold wet, freezing bunch of dog face GI's that finally slog into welcome streets of Montigny, secured hours earlier by our 2nd & 3rd Battalions. The fading light of late afternoon glints off the wet cobblestones as our billeting party locates our HQ and home for the night.

It is a large, upstairs, barracks sized room loaded with the cheery glow of red hot, cast iron stoves radiating heat everywhere. What a welcome sight for this bunch of "Sad Sacks." Shortly the whole place is a mass of soaking-wet, 2-ton wool overcoats, combat fatigue jackets and pants, boots, socks, underwear and gear... all mixed in with their soggy owners.

This menagerie is hung out to dry, draped at crazy angles, as close to the stoves as each guy can get his stuff. Ultimately this sheer bedlam subsides as everyone and everything slowly begins to warm up and thaw out. We chow down and in the wee hours layout the bed rolls and crash for the night... each soul trying to put his thoughts of the day's disastrous events behind him. Exhaustion finally prevails, and all sink into a sound sleep, much needed for what lies ahead.

Our bedtime experiences on the nights of 15-16 Nov. are a case in point. For analogy: Case [1] listed above: The cold wet day in November.

The typical hole in the mud dug by our 2nd squad is a slit trench as described above, with one neat additional neat feature added: Each hole for a bed has 3-4" of water in the bottom. Now, pilgrim, get your creativity in gear this one... How do you keep your whole bottom half out of the water, all night long?!

For the creative mind the answer is simple: cut up two bushels of saplings and sticks about ¼ " diameter in various lengths, arrange them in a cross-pattern matrix near the bottom of the slit trench. Then, wedge the strongest main sticks into the mud on the sides, just above the water level, and then keep piling on the sticks until they support your weight. Presto... a dandy bed for the night, when one is not out on patrol.

Chapter Eight - Part D
Crossing the Vezouze River, flowing through Lake Gresson

Now back to the fray. During black night hours, 0200-0500 Thurs.16 Nov... Our 1st Battalion sends out patrols attempting to cross the Vezouze River, flowing through Lake Gresson. We are stopped first by a German tank, and then later in the day by MG fire on both our flanks.

16 Nov. it is reported that during the night our phone lines were cut by the enemy into pieces 20-50 feet long, while they continue to pound our Battalion area with heavy incomings of artillery & mortar fire. We take 30 German prisoners during the day.

The enemy continues their harassing artillery fire on key road junctions through the night of 16 Nov. and the early morning hours of 17 November, followed by substantial increase in intensity as the day goes on. At one time our platoon of TD's becomes exposed and bango, immediately gets a 120-round blast... 88 mm's high velocity, flat trajectory, (German AA gun).

Our 3rd Battalion sends out fruitless patrols to find a gap in the enemy lines. These Krauts sure do not want to report to Hitler that they have been pushed back through the Saverne Gap! This is to be their last big stand before the final rout to come. Our persistence pays off however, and before dawn we finally overrun an enemy outpost managing to get half of Co. (80 guys) across the lousy Lake Gresson river (the Vezouze) before daylight. This, only to be halted by a humongous German barrage of everything they have, preventing a bridgehead expansion.

Sunday 19 Nov. dawns with continued enemy fire all day long, but it is becoming less effective. This is due undoubtedly to the sub-par German G2, not knowing just where in the heck these dang Americans are deployed. An attempt by friendly troops to advance in area just off the east of Harbouey with tanks is met with heavy concentrations of fire including howitzers.

Finally, our 1st Battalion departs our beloved "Bivouac on the Sticks" under harassing fire, with our sights set on the town of Tanconville. We cannot help but discern that enemy resistance is starting to crack.

This fight clearly has not been easy or quick. The soggy terrain in the Lake Gresson valley doesn't help much. Such is our life in the two days it takes to clear the Lake Gresson area.

Chapter Eight - Part E
Big Blue 79 moves on Blamont & Harbouey Ridge
Dateline: **Tuesday-Thursday, 14-16 November 1944 - Onto Halloville & Harbouey**
These are the Axis of the Battle. The Big Blue 79 advances on Central Halloville, Harbouey, and Lake Gresson, Just south of Tanconville. The 314th Reg. to the north, in the vicinity of Barbas and Blamont; The 315 deployed down the middle; 313th deployed to the south. The battle axis is out of Montigny, through St Pole, and Bandonviller, and Montreux. We are facing the German 708th Inf. Div. In heavy fighting we drive in a deep wedge almost cutting them in half.

Ultimately this is to set the stage for the German withdrawal becoming a route! This in turn is to enable the French 2nd Armored advance through the Vosges into Strasbourg. What part does our 1st Battalion have to do with all of this? We are smack in the middle of the whole deal!

Chapter Eight - Part F
First Battalion assault on Halloville
Dateline: **Wednesday 15 November 1944- Our first combat stack of WW2**

It is indeed appropriate here that this story be told both from the perspective of the civilians involved, and that of the American GI's ...a rare treatment in most WW2 books.

It is 0700 Tuesday morning 14 Nov. Just to the east of Montigny, Company "A" of the 813th TD's Tank Destroyers) and Company "B" of the 749th Tank Battalion (Sherman Tanks) resume their attack on Ancerviller. They are assisted by the 2nd Battalion of the 315th who, after some, severe house-to-house fighting, complete the capture and liberate the town by day's end.

Concurrently our 3rd Battalion clears out St. Pole to the south. In the meantime, our 1st Battalion, now dried out at Montigny, bypasses Ancerviller on the north side and pushes up to the hills and high ground to the NW of Halloville. Here we dig foxholes for the night. We dig them right, as evidenced by the fact that those holes are still there upon the 1996 West Family return trip to Halloville.

Wednesday morning 15 Nov. the full Battalion echelon attack on Halloville is scheduled for 0730. At 0700 this correspondent takes stock of the view from our jump off position in the clearing just to the south of our bivouac in the woods.

The attack route is across an immense, open field of harvested corn, sloping down to the SE over a mile to the German positions in Halloville. There is no cover in the field and the attack formation is to be awesome (shock and awe of 1944): A full Battalion moving abreast at a fast walk with about 10 feet apart.

That is 1000 GI's all shooting from the hip a virtual hail of suppression fire into every square inch of Halloville real estate. They are all shooting semi-automatic (Mls) and fully automatic (BARs) in short bursts, continuously as they walk forward down into town. It is the only tactic that will work attacking across open fields. Without this suppression fire, German defensive machine guns could and would simply decimate our attack formation. I would not want to be on the receiving end of this suppression fire.

One other thing (I recalled only after prompting in 1996): Sgt. Cone briefs our squad as do all the other squad leaders in the entire Battalion. It is blood curdling. His order is for us to scream, yell, and holler out a stream of "Geronimo" shouts... at the top of our lungs, as loud as we can. This is ontop of the staccato of the automatic fire, all the way into Halloville. And at 0730 hours we do indeed make Geronimo proud!

The attack begins, supported by Tanks and TD's. We face heavy small arms, flat trajectory & artillery fire from defending Krauts. It is to be an all-day attack. Five enemy tanks and other vehicles are destroyed. We take 91 prisoners, along with equipment.

Chapter Eight - Part G
A graphic civilian perspective at the face of war
Dateline: November 1-15 1944 - The Jacques Chronicles

Now time to switch perspectives... from attacking GI's to that of the civilians on the receiving end of all of this hail of fire. But we need to back up to 1 Nov. 1944 to our rest days in Bayonne to set the stage for this remarkable, first-hand account by Michael Jacques.

He was 15 yrs. old at the liberation of Halloville... only 4 years younger than this soldier correspondent, I have to say. On the occasion of our 1996 family visit to re-trace the Liberation Battle Route, as all ten of us Americans approached Halloville from the SW in two minivans my mind was churning. We simply had no clue of what to expect.

I agonized and quizzed: In this town "How in creation can anyone still be alive and even begin to recall the events of 15 November 1944? (The day I stormed into the town with my BAR) My query was surely answered quickly.

The entire town had turned out and assembled at the Church yard. We had interpreters on both sides. Wow! Did they remember... you have to be kidding! They had just regained 4 long years of lost freedom. Shortly, you will understand why. The face of war... you had to ask!

Chapter Eight - Part H
The Jacques Chronicles - Liberation of Halloville; Written and privately issued by Michel Jacques and his brother Pierre, July 1997. Events of Nov. 5, 1944.

"Halloville, a small village of 100, is situated about 4 Km south of Blamont. Since November 1 the front line is stabilized on a Montigny, Migneville, Herbeviller. All the frontline villages have been evacuated. The Krauts had moved the JACQUES family away from Migneville to Halloville on 16 October. Now they sought refuge from the Germans in a deserted farm on the outskirts of Halloville along the road to Ancerviller.

Then, on November 8, all the men from Ancerviller are gathered and forcibly moved to Germany. The rest of the population is similarly evacuated, Friday November 10. We could see all of these people passing in front of our house with racks pulled by themselves. These contained cows, chickens, and a little bit of cherished furniture. It is a sad and devastating scene, but it is typical at the face of war.

On Saturday 11 November all the men, ages 16-55, are to be gathered in front of the church to be moved to an undisclosed location. Luckily it was raining very heavily on that day, and a new German military order was issued postponing the first one. On Sunday 12 November the day is calm, but the shelling of Halloville is starting and lasts all night. It is real fireworks!

All calibers of high explosive (HE) and phosphorus artillery shells totally illuminate the country-side. My father and my brother are slaughtering a pig in the backyard of our house. I am about to join them when an artillery shell explodes on the scene. Luckily a 2-meter wall protects us and we are hit by only a few pieces of roof on our heads. Not needing any further motivation, we head right back to the cellar, in short order.

On Monday13 November the artillery shelling of Halloville continues sporadically, but we don't leave the cellar much this day. In the afternoon we hear machine guns in Ancerviller as it is liberated by the 2nd Battalion of the 315th.

On Tuesday morning 14 November my uncle Robert from Ancerviller who had just escaped from a German-held group of fellow villager prisoners, arrives at our house. He asks my father if he could come along with him to join his family refuges over in Cirey sur Vezouze. Over my mother's objections, my father agrees, takes the horses and the rack, and leaves with my uncle.

As the shelling increases along the way they literally fly across Nonhigny. A shell landed on the church and my uncle's foot was cut by a piece of shrapnel. The rest of the trip goes without incident.

The return trip to Halloville is worse, because in the meantime. the Americans had advanced and were now north of Ancerviller-Hameau. On the Barbas-Nonhigny road, my father turns off, heading for Halloville. 1st Bo. GIs see him in an area where civilians are not supposed to be running around.

In Luneville they had learned the hard way that French civilians are often used as artillery spotters, by the Germans guys who can cost hundreds of American lives. So, it isn't easy to tell friend from foe in the fog of war. Hesitation can get GIs killed, and accordingly, my father is mistaken for the enemy and the Americans bring machine gun and artillery fire to bear on him. In the thick of war now, bullets are whistling above his head and an artillery round lands in front of him.

Two men, who happen to be under fire in the nearby ditch, try to see if my father is hurt. It turns out that he is lucky this day and escapes injury (One of these is later to become my father in law). He goes on to the first farmhouse and stops overnight, unable under fire to return to his own house. He spends the night in the cellar of my uncle.

Tuesday 14 November the raging battle continues on, and at the end of the afternoon, my uncle's house where we have taken refuge is invaded by retreating German troops. One German soldier, sent to find a way out for them, comes back a few minutes later soaking wet. He had to jump into a river to escape American bullets.

Promptly reporting to his officers, they don't allow him to change clothes until he finishes the German debriefing, 15 minutes later. He asks my mother to give him dry clothes and she does so with obvious pity for him. She even gives him a cup of hot coffee as an added bonus. The rains continue to pour… so much lately, the water is flooding my uncle's cellar and others everywhere. So now we move *again* to a neighbor's house.

So it is that on the night of 14 November my family is separated into three groups in Halloville: my father at my uncles' place; my (other) brother and sister at the neighbor's house; finally my mother, brother and I stay at still another house in an un-flooded corner of the cellar."

Chapter Eight - Part I
The stage is now set for the epic battle of Halloville (An intermission in the Michel Jacques story)

The reader is asked to conjure up this priceless image of two Jacques brothers, Michael, 15 and Pierre, 17, huddled in an un-flooded corner of a cellar. In 1996 we are told that they do *what all kids are told not to do...* daring to peer out a cellar window at what?

Yet another teenager, this correspondent, a 19-year-old American. He is part of the 1000 man, "Geronimo" hoard of shouting GI's described above. The brothers brace themselves for the shock and awe of the incoming suppression barrage of what? Perhaps 30,000 rounds (minimum) of automatic weapon fire, shredding and decimating the houses, walls, windows and courtyards of Halloville.

Now let's continue with the fascinating story by this French family. Fox News is not there in 1944. But young Michel Jacques is there, and we owe him a lot for this authentic first-hand, historical record, rare indeed in the saga of WW2. It is liberation day for Halloville:

"Wednesday 15 Nov. starts off with a very loud wake-up call that rattles and humbles everyone (French and Germans alike). I dare having to look out (a cellar window). From upstairs, just above our heads, comes the thunder of German officers stomping all over the floor and shouting orders *very loudly*. Soldiers are running all over the place just outside, taking positions behind trees and wood piles.

I am back in the cellar as the American attack starts. A German soldier is posted just outside the cellar window, shooting sporadically. Then, after about a half hour the initial high intensity barrage is slowing down. I come up the stairs to look out through a first-floor window. I can see two German soldiers hidden together in a corner of our neighbor's house. I return to the cellar thinking the Americans cannot be very far away now.

Then suddenly we hear very loud noises in our refuge house... grenades, explosions, firing bursts from machines along with loud shouting. I tell my mother that they're going to throw grenades into the cellar! Alarmed, we quickly come up the stairway Shouting "Civilian"… "Civilian" at the top of our lungs. My mother opens the door and the kitchen is full of American soldiers. Very surprised to see civilians they point their guns at us.

They ask us if there are any German soldiers left in the house. They then take my brother (Pierre?) and carefully visit every room in the house... with him in front of them. Our "house liberator" soldiers then go outside and we follow them up to the barn door. We then witness the arrival of another group of American Soldiers about 10 meters away.

Suddenly there is a tremendous explosion in our midst. A German tank from the lower part of the village fires a main gun round (75 or 88 millimeters?) directly at our refuge house. The shell breaks right through the kitchen window and explodes in the corridor next to the barn. Paint and debris from the corridor wall comes down on our heads.

We retreat rapidly to the cellar as a second tank round thunders into our refuge house and explodes in the back room of the house. Nobody is hurt, but it was very close! After about another half hour the battle tempo seems to cool down a bit, so I tell my mother, "I will go and see what has happened to my young brothers after all of this mayhem. The battle scene is ugly."

I see a dead German soldier killed right in front of the house facing ours. Checking out the cellar there… what a surprise!! It is full of German Soldiers (live ones). I explain to the landlord, who is an Alsatian and can speak very good German, that the Americans are in Halloville in huge numbers. A thousand in a village of 100.

While the Alsatian was updating the German soldiers on their status, I venture outside and tell two American soldiers, who are walking down the road with two prisoners, that this house was full of

Germans. Prudently, they decline to go in, but - surprise! As we were still talking, the whole cellar full of Germans soldiers comes out, hands up. They surrender also and join the two.

Now the lower half of Halloville is liberated. My father comes back home and together we survey the aftermath of the battle. Losses are heavy on both sides. Two German tanks are burned out and destroyed next to the milk factory... the bodies of their crews all torn apart (by the incoming shells that destroyed the tanks) and strewn everywhere. I also see a truck passing by, full of American cadavers.

The French 2nd Armored Division under the command of Morel Deville arrive in Halloville just before 1200 hours. The streets are littered with (broken) equipment of all kinds: Jeeps, machine guns, tanks, and cannons, but, wow, we are so happy to finally see our French Troops.

By the end of the afternoon, the American Troops (1st Battalion of the 315th) go on to liberate Harbouey which we can see burning in the event. On Thursday 16 November the Americans liberate Nonhigny, then Bandonviller, and finally Blamont on 18 November. In the aftermath a few artillery batteries of the retreating Germans are still shooting up to 8 days later.

Two German shells (rounds) land at the crossroads between Ancerviller, Nonhigny and Halloville, killing one inhabitant just trying to get back home. I am also the victim of similar explosions, peppering my legs with stones while I am trying to fill up buckets of water at the fountain. Finally, we return to Halloville very happy to find our house in a sad state, but that we can still live in it." *Michel Jacques, July 1997.*

Chapter Eight - Part J
A snapshot of the 2ⁿᵈ Squad, 2ⁿᵈ Platoon, Baker Co.

At this point it is appropriate to introduce the guys with whom I am fighting, working, and living on the line in Alsace-Lorraine.

Our great Squad Leader, Staff Sgt. Gerry Cone, 22, is from just north of Syracuse, NY State. He is a small joe, about 5'5", medium build, wearing a perpetual grin. Sideling along with a weed hanging out of his mouth... my first impression is wow, there is a sly 'silent sam.' Says little but knows a heck of a lot... a real suave guy!

Actually, he is as much of a kid as any of us... gets things done without getting tough about it. He, like the entire squad, has an everlasting sense of humor...used to drive a big semi-truck rig all through the New York State.

Gerry is one of the very few original men left that shipped through Camp Phillips, Kansas, with the Division. He has been fighting continually since 0+6 and hasn't been hit yet!! In Bayonne he offered me the second in command job with a buck Sgt. rating... which I wisely turned down, never to regret it.

Harry Balantine is another good egg... really has had a rough civilian life and is part of the microcosm of teenagers who, in 1944-45 salvaged civilization for all of us today. And now, in 2007, they *are doing it again* for a dubious, and ungrateful America who haven't yet learned the fundamental lessons of history and freedom. He had to quit school around the 5th grade to start working. From there he knocked around construction jobs until he was drafted. From Warren, Ohio, he came in as a replacement before I did, and God bless him, immediately started to buck for 3 stripes (Buck Sgt.). When he finally got them, you should have seen this guy... tickled like a kid with a new toy! His name is Harry, but we all call him George (don't know why). So, there you have it, our Asst. Squad Leader, 20 years old, face of a kid and a head of curly brown hair.

Don Weiskopff, 19, of Buffalo, New York is not part of the Lorraine campaign. He came in as a replacement about 0+30, went back to the hospital with bum feet and then came back to join our squad around 24 December. Near Riedseltz he becomes my assistant BAR man in our Super foxhole Deluxe. He later really does become the BAR man after I am hit. He goes on to tell an incredible story in the Rittershoffen and Hatten Saga to follow. A long, lean, lanky guy about 6'3" with a round face and a big round grin to match, he is a funny guy... always joking about something.

"Pete" and "Mexico" are an inseparable pair, a two-man rifle team in our 12-man squad. Readers first hear of them in the Friendly Fire KIA saga. "Pete" is a black-eyed, black-haired Spaniard from Puerto Rico, speaks broken English with a really funny accent. He can be spotted a mile away, his teeth showing bright white underneath a black mustache. Pete is 24, four years older than his buddy "Mexico." The two of them get together in big Spanish Pow-wows. The zum-zum voice of Pete is like a walking boogie beat, blending with Mexico's higher pitched voice. And get this... they sing, for hours at a time, a complete repertoire of Spanish/Mexican songs… "La cook-a-racha ... Pas-a-Ia-mucho. Pete is about 5'7", built light. Mexico is plump like an Eskimo. He was born and raised in the home of Texas A&M University, Bryan Texas, of Mexican parents.

With this touch of humanity added to the reader's perception of a WW2 fighting squad at the face of war... we now rejoin the fray.

Chapter Eight - Part K
Blamont- Lake Gresson -Tanconville Campaign
Dateline: Thurs-Sun. 16-19 Nov. 1944 - Harbouey & Fromonville to Tanconville

Division picture: To the north the Big Blue 79 is gradually encircling Blamont in this time frame, setting the stage for a complete German rout through the Saverne Gap. Just to the ESE, the 314th and 315th Regiments are clearing out the Harbouey Ridge in the Lake Gresson area, with sights set on Tanconville. On 16-17 November, just to the south, in the town of Barbas, our 315th 3rd Battalion is cutting off the roads leading north into Blamont.

An estimated 300 enemy infantry and four tanks flee north into Blamont in this engagement. In this same sector our 314th Regiment encounters some difficulty. The Big Blue 79, is to be bombarded by nightmare German artillery barrages while trying to fix a bridge blown by the retreating Germans. Our 304th Engineer Battalion support it by laying down a "treadway" bridge. Ultimately, they're to complete the bridge with the support of our counter artillery.

Crucial to XV Corps strategy, the enemy is forced to fall back each night. The German retreat in the face the 44th & 79th Div. assault finally turns into a full-blown rout.

This, readers, is just one day in the life of a "Combat Team" in 1944... at work to secure your freedom in 2007. Learn to appreciate both it and the brave souls who make it happen. Young civilian teenager Jean Mohler (507), is tromping all over his native Blamont, trying to stay alive in the total mayhem of war.

This is just as his friend Michael Jacques does in Halloville; Jean, of Marcy L'Etoile is devoting his life to writing his book on the Blamont Liberation.

An attempt by friendly troops to advance in the wooded area just south of Cirey sur Vezouze, and east of Harbouey with tanks is met with particularly heavy concentrations of fire including howitzers.

Despite this our 3rd Battalion crosses the Vezouze under cover of darkness. Part of "L" Co. spear heads this advance, establishing a bridgehead... the rest of the 3rd Battalion to follow. Again, the Germans pound this bridgehead as well, but with much less steam than yesterday. Our 2nd Battalion follows suit. Finally, our 1st Bo. departs our beloved "Bivouac on the Sticks".

This is done under harassing fire, with our sights set on the town of Tanconville. We cannot help but discern that enemy resistance is starting to crack.

Chapter Eight - Part L
Tanconville
Dateline: Sat. and Sun., 18 and 19 November 1944

Saturday is spent in transit from the Lake Gresson marsh, through Cirey to the Tanconville vicinity. Early Sunday, 19 November our 1st Battalion sends out a combat patrol that finds many abandoned German positions along with a bevy of new equipment, hastily abandoned in their retreat. With this stark evidence of the German withdrawal.

The 1st Battalion CP closes in on Tanconville during the day. East of Tanconville our 79th Div. Recon Troop locates three pill boxes that are quickly taken out by 613th TD Battalion. Enemy fire picks up on our 1st Battalion. But the enemy is quickly mopped up with Capt. Ray Harvey's "A" Co. leading the way They go on to capture a German Aid Station, intact with its horse and cart.

The 2nd and 3rd Battalions follow under harassing enemy fire in the vicinity of Fremonville to the SW. The Germans begin their general withdrawal at 2000 hours and continue through the night. They abandon much equipment which we capture. So clearly now our march to the Rhine continues at an accelerated pace. The GIs of 315th Regiment are making history with each step taken.

Chapter Eight - Part M
Niderhoff
Dateline: Mon.20 Nov.1944

Trek on the Liberation Battle Route continues Sunday night the Big Blue 79 order comes down for a major move by the 315th.

The evidence is now clear that the Germans are headed for a Saverne Gap withdrawal. Time to shake loose our armor, so the French 2nd Armored Division is given the green light to lead the way. At 0730 our 1st Battalion moves out on foot from Tanconville but are slowed by congested roads, closing in on Niderhoff at 1730 where we join the Reg. CP.

Chapter Eight - Part N
Hartzviller
Dateline: Tues 21 Nov.1944 - Huge delays due to 2nd Armor move

Biding our time in Niderhoff most of the day Tues, we finally are released to move at 1415, closing in on Hartzviller at 1700. Baker Co. assigns this correspondent to the billeting party. For the first time in eons we are to sleep in warm houses.

Chapter Eight - Part O
Arzviller and St. Louis
Dateline: **Wed. 22 Nov.1944 - Blown bridge forces Detour**

At 0700 our 1st Battalion departs Hartzviller by foot and motor to Arzviller, under enemy small arms and mortar fire. The CP closes in at Arzwiller at 1100, and later moves on to St. Louis at 1545. At 0500 the enemy had blown a large bridge in the vicinity of Arzviller.

This forced the 2nd Armored to detour under enemy harassing fire. On the way to Arzwiller, 1st Battalion engages and eliminates this force with the help of direct fire from TDs. The enemy riflemen are using caves and overhanging ledges for firing positions, and those bypassed continued sniping at our GIs, maintaining close contact with us through late at night. Meanwhile our 2nd Battalion continues moving eastward on the north side of the canal in the vicinity of Henridorf, still in enemy hands. All day Wed. 22 Nov. the Germans continued their costly retreat. Their rear-guard action is to give us fits. They create new roadblocks by blasting trees across the roads. Our Cannon Co. and supporting 904th Field Artillery Battalion, in turn, blast away at the German Woodchoppers.

Chapter Eight - Part P
Thanksgiving in Lutzelbourg
Dateline: **Thurs. 23 Nov.1944 Total blackout Turkey dinner from Co mess Jeep**

At 1430 our 1st Battalion moves forward to Lutzelbourg, closing in at 1645 in total darkness. Our billeting party puts us in houses along the main drag of Lutzelbourg.

Not only is it an absolutely pitch dark, moonless night, but also straggler rear guard Nazi soldiers and snipers are everywhere, just looking for a chance to kill more American GIs.

Hence, we are in a 100% black-out alert. Not even a sliver of light can sneak out of any house in town. Snug in our home for the night most of us take immediate advantage of this rare opportunity to catch up on our ever-present deluge of mail call.

Our little abode is scattered with GIs huddled with candles under shielding blankets, reading and writing letters. We are also hungry (as usual) and are expecting the Baker Company Mess Jeep at any time. This soldier, pen in hand, is in the middle of a word, when about 1900 hours we hear the loudest clatter and rumbling outside in the pitch-black street.

What else could this be but the friendly guys from our Company Kitchen! At this clear alarm I drop my pen, snuff out my candle, grab my mess kit and follow the hoard of chowhounds invading the street. There is simply no way to navigate except by sound and smell, so there is a lot of stumbling, bumbling, collisions and cussing on the Lutzelbourg cobblestones this night.

The first to catch my attention are the muffled voices of our kitchen staff giving instructions and trying to keep some semblance of order out of pure chaos. Next is the plop, plop, plop of food being dumped into mess kits, along with the steam, sizzle, swish and of hot coffee dumping into huge canteen cups.

Mind you, we cannot see a darn thing! Not the servers, not our mess kits, and sure as heck, not what kind of chow is being dumped into them… but the aroma, lord almighty, the aroma, wafting through the night air, along with the idle lazy currents of warm steam are something else! Enough to stir the soul of any solid American Dog Face.

The mess line is formed by the lead mess jeep, and a long string of trailers, each specializing in the various food and beverage groups. My turn comes. I hold out my mess kit, hear the plop and feel the increase the weight, without the slightest clue of what it is… only the smell gives me a clue. Same with my canteen cup as it overflows! This is because the KP guys, even with their temporarily endowed, radar eyes, cannot tell when it is full, until I yell "say when!"

Stumbling back to our abode, it is an amazing scene of enlightenment, as a packed room of GI's, mind you by candlelight, finally see what is in their kits and cups. The most sumptuous, steaming hot, Thanksgiving Dinner ever cooked and served to any GI anywhere… anyplace! Keep in mind, this is going on all over the war fronts of WW2.

CHAPTER NINE

The Alsace Campaign. South of Moder River and Haguenau

PREFACE REMARKS: The action timeline for this chapter covers the period 24 November through 15 December 1944. The primary source documents are war letters written 63 years ago. WW2 is raging everywhere. It is 5.5 months after D-Day Normandy.

Chapter Nine - Part A
Liberation convoy, launched from Lutzelbourg, (the ride of our lives on top of the leading TD -tank destroyer)

It is 0800, Friday morning as Sgt. Gerry Cone bursts into the room where our 2nd Squad had sacked out after our fabulous turkey dinner, "OK boys-grab your junk and get it "on the-ready" to move out any time now. He has just come from the 2nd Platoon CP with the inevitable "move out" order in Army life. And... he has mail, a couple of Stars and Stripes newspapers, and our three K-Rations apiece.

As is usually the case when move-out orders come down this soldier correspondent has all of his writin' stuff spread all around a candle on the table. I snatch it all up and stash it in the left pocket of my combat jacket. Our equipment ready, the entire squad pushes everyone else out of available candle-light in the effort to read the new incoming letters.

The Sergeant has that special grin on his face. We can tell he is up to something. He is lugging a bazooka (a rocket firing tube about 3" diameter x 4' long) on his shoulder. He sidles up to ol' "Slotnick," a 25-year-old Polish, nudging him with the tube in the ribs. Not a word is spoken.

Then ol' Slotnick explodes "Ko-avay, don't bother me with such stuff!"

Not taking his eyes off his letter he mutters disgustingly, "If you tink I'm going to carry dot ting, yoo're plum krayzee… itz too hefv."

I sigh to myself with relief, I'm glad I have the BAR. It weighs in at 35 lbs. with ammo. No way can he also make me carry the bazooka with any try. Not when another all-day road march is likely. But poor ol' Slotnick is elected it seems…Ol' Bazooka-man Slotnick!

Interjection: Can you imagine in your wildest dreams a Nazi Sgt. giving an order as above? Chances are nil to zero. This is what distinguishes the American from the German Army.

Slotnick staggers out into the street where "Nick" (as we called T/Sgt. Nixon, our Platoon Sgt.) is forming our Platoon. He mutters in Polish as he goes and knocking down everything in his way with the clumsy steel tube.

The town is sure alive with troops and vehicles this cool, snappy morning. Our squad moves by a whole mess of newly arrived rear-echelon troops, and gripe about those lucky jokers. Then our 1st Battalion splits off to form a column. Our feet are hollering up at us, "If you think you're going to make us tramp-tramp-tramp on the road all day again today… you're crazy."

Just then as we head up an alleyway the situation changes. We hear the powerful drone and thunder of diesel engines warming up! Out in a lot, amidst clouds of blue smoke loom five big, beautiful babies of the 813th TD Bn (Tank Destroyer Battalion). Spontaneously our feet explode with the ear shattering cheer "Happy days in the Foothills !!!" We concur. We are going to ride on TD's today!!! Now comes irrepressible Slotnick's moment of triumph, "Ah Ha - you beeg lug, Cone… Vat did I tell you, about dot Klumzee bazooka. HA! Von beegjoke on you- huh? Beeg Tank going to carry dot no goot thing now!"

Only when this soldier correspondent is comfortably perched on the aft end, behind the 76mm main gun turret of one of those angels from heaven did he begin to believe it. The Dog Faces are being mechanized for this one day out of the year. Like the Lone Ranger's, "We are off in a cloud of dust, smoke and the flash of sputtering exhaust." We feel a wonderful surge of power underneath us… that grinding vibration that only tank tracks can produce. Now get this… we are the lead TD at the point of the 315th Reg. long motorized column.

This has to be GI Doughfoot's day of triumph and exhilaration beyond belief. Snug, warm and comfortable, the turret breaking the wind, with bodily fatigue fading into history. Without sweating brow and aching feet he can now gaze down on town populace with an air and spirit of the true Liberation of Lorraine and Western Alsace.

Starting from Saverne we are eastbound for Wahlenheim, south of the Moder in our next battle zone. We rumble through village after village along the Marne au Rhin Canal, (and 1996 route D421). Some of the liberated villages along the way are: Dettwiller, Wilwisheim, Melsheim, Hochfelder, and Mommenheim, just SW of Wahlenheim.

Every single one of these villages greets us with the most tumultuous ovation I have ever believed possible. I wish the half of 2007 America, who believe the trash that the USA never does anything right, could have been there. They have short memories.

Our entire 315th TD column is literally showered with apples, pears, peaches, and bouquets of flowers of all kinds. Brightly clad peasant congregations, hundreds to a group, crowded the street corners, some far from their homes. They are waving hats, throwing hats, and hollering at the top of their lungs "Viva la America"

The younger set lined up in battery formation on both sides of our TD's are heaving apples from huge baskets. They heave them in rapid fire, like baseballs (I kid you not) with uncanny accuracy at the simply overwhelmed American GIs on the TDs. We catch and devour as many as we can, and our steel helmets save us from the rest. Many underestimate the speed of our TD's and the fruit falls behind us.

Some of the tiny ones, the worry-wart kids hide their heads under their mother's aprons. Some scamper back in the doorways as the terrible rumble of our tank treads thunder by. On a few occasions the column comes to a jerky halt. Then the crowd really closes in on us with all variety of food and drink, wine, cognac, hot milk, bread and jelly.

I joke and talk with them in broken German. Their story is universally the same. For four long years under the Nazi Jack Boot., the "Bosche" (Germans) have taken everything and given nothing in return. They have forced men, women and children to dig their foxholes and defensive trenches around town. They have shot or hung those who would not work as forced labor.

I have listened to these proud Alsatians talk for hours around lamp lit tables in their wood range kitchens, belaboring what the Bosche did to them. First-hand stuff. Well, our day of glory is about to come to an abrupt end as we again hit a Kraut stronghold up ahead. One half of 2007 America, please listen up and consider something precious *you have never lost*. The above is what happens when proud people lose their freedom for five years... *and then regain it.*

Chapter Nine - Part B
Regimental convoy billeting party in the South Moder
Dateline: **Fri.24 Nov.1944. Saverne departure to the new Battle of the Moder**

Regimental Picture: Early in the morning up through noon time the enemy continues to retreat through the Saverne pass with elements of the 315th Reg. in hot pursuit. German rear-guard elements reek all the havoc they can with prepared demolition charges along the way. Obviously, the forced Nazi retreat, eastbound along Route D421 gives Alsatian townsfolk new hope. From Dettwiller to Mommenheim, this retreat is a "preview of coming attractions" along this road. They no doubt watch with suppressed glee, from hidden positions, as the hated Bosche move to new defensive positions south of the Moder River.

The Regimental Billeting Party departs very early at 0415 bound for the new CP location planned for Rottelsheim. Both the former Mayor and the present Nazi Mayor had not fled, talks with them are underway, just as a German force is spotted attacking Rottelsheim from the north., The Billeting party that is now obliged to withdraw to Bernolsheim, just to the west.

Later in the day at 1300 the 315th Liberation Convoy departs Saverne with Baker Company assigned as the leading company. After the all-day convoy ride, they arrive in the South Moder area, dismount and, with Able Company, re-engage the Germans in the Rottelsheim area against small arms and some mortar fire.

Chapter Nine - Part C
Lead tank destroyers of the 1ˢᵗ Battalion arrive in Wahlenheim
Dateline: **Fri. 24 Nov. 1944 - The Celebration is over…time to fight again.**

It is 2050 hours and dark as the lead Tank Destroyers carrying Baker Company close in on Rottelsheim, just east of Wahlenheim.

We dismount from our lead TD (the very first in line) and ol' Slotnick now has to carry the bazooka! We take up positions to secure the high ground north of Rottelsheim, while the Regimental CP is set up in Wahlheim under cover of darkness.

At 2210 air bursts and mortar fire are taken by the 1st Battalion moving through Mommenheim. The next morning of Saturday 25 November arrives in relative calm after the stirring events of yesterday's liberation convoy. However, in the next three days, 26-28 Nov, the entire Haguenau sector is turned into an explosive cauldron of night firefights as the Germans make their stand on the Moder River Line.

Regimental Picture: During the night Saturday 25 November the Regiment receives some harassing artillery/AA fire and the enemy is active with recon (reconnaissance) patrols and heavily mining the roads west and south out of Kriegsheim. The 3rd Battalion attacks this German stronghold with many casualties. On Sunday 26 Nov. our recon patrols are very active!

We learn that the Wehrmacht is committed to making a heavy stand in the South Moder. Enemy troops have been pouring into the sector, arriving by train over three days, detraining in Haguenau and Bischwiller, elements of the German 256th Division. On Monday 27 November our recon patrols indicate the enemy is occupying Davendorf, Ohlungen, Batzendorf and Niederschaeffolsheim. Our work is cut out for us, and the first in line is a big one, Batzendorf.

Chapter Nine – Part D
Battle of Batzendorf
Dateline: **Tues-Wed.28-29 Nov. 44 - Teenage GI Bob Shane is KIA**

In the early morning of 26 Nov. Bob Shane and I along with our 1st. Battalion Baker Co. 1st Platoon buddies are dug in the open pasture just east of Wahlenheim, about a mile or so south of Batzendorf. Tues. 28 Nov. the 1st Battalion CO sets the attack H-Hour for 1200. The battle continues all day. The town is captured at 0900 on the 29th 1st Battalio. CP in at 1130. There follows this correspondent's best recollection of this horrendous battle. Burp Guns are German automatic assault rifles with a 1000 round per minute fire rate, so fast that individual rounds cannot be distinguished... only a continuous "Burrp" at 17 rounds per second!! One can easily distinguish the pow-pow-pow-pow- sound of automatic fire coming from our slow firing BAR's at about 250-300 rounds per minute, or 4-5 rounds per second.

In the wee hours of 27-28 November, the night air is lit up and punctuated by Nazi Burp Gun fire all around our positions from every direction. It is 0600, 28 Nov. when the Batzendorf attack order is issued. The entire 79th Division is committed to the attack. It begins at high noon (315th on the left, 314th on the right, and 313th in reserve). The117th Cav. to secure the Div. flank right flank... the attack plan for the 315th Reg. Our 1st Battalion on the right, 2nd on the left and 3rd in reserve.

Nach sechs und vierzig jahren das kommt mir nicht auf dem zin! Translation: After 46 yrs., this story is difficult to retrieve in my noggin!

As a single soldier correspondent my recollection of the mayhem that ensues is fuzzy at best after 60 years. Baker company is set up to provide flanking fire along a long, crescent shaped arc of high ground, overlooking the open pasture valley. Our squad is dug in at one end of the arc and Bob Shane's squad is dug in at the other end. This valley separates us from the Nazi defense line they hold around

Batzendorf. Other 1st Battalion resources are involved for the direct assault on the town. Our flanking fire is to cover and support them to the hilt with every tracer we can pour in there.

Well, all hell breaks loose that night as an intense firefight lights up the entire sky above the village & at least 180 degrees round it. M-1 Rifle. BAR & Burp Gun tracer fire crisscross the pasture from us about every conceivable direction and elevation.

It is a long, lousy night of pandemonium & horror with an ungodly amount of un-aimed, but sprayed ammunition expended. The attack goes on all afternoon and all night on the 28th• But in the end Batzendorf is captured at 0900 on the 29th. I only vaguely recall getting some kind of sleep in my hole after things settled down.

A grey and bitter cold dawn slides over the valley and our positions along the crescent shaped ridge! The move out order comes down. Mexico, Slotnick, Weiskopff and I collect our gear and start around the ridge toward the positions of Bob Shane's squad. Along with all of the other GIs we move past evacuated foxholes that had been so busy the night before. Our first clue that something is wrong came as we noted one BAR man still in his hole in firing position at the far end of the line. Sharp pangs of apprehension, fear and doubt would be mild understatements characterizing the thoughts racing through our heads as we closed in on that position: The last time I saw Bob Shane.

An image comes into focus that leaves us speechless, silent and prayerful as we move up the rise leading to that foxhole. I walk slowly up toward that now silent BAR at about 45 degrees off the barrel azimuth. There is that humongous flash hider, about 75 caliber, a 3/4" diameter cylinder, 4" long, on the end of the muzzle.

It is still pointed aggressively across the valley pasture at the German positions of the night before. Just behind the flash hider is the bipod supporting the barrel on the freezing mud, just in front of the foxhole, parapet.

With a reverence and despair that still defies words and humanity, I reach out & touch the cold steel barrel and look straight into the face of Bob Shane. It is just one image, among hundreds, burned into my brain for 60 years this writing… surfacing lately beyond control. It is the usual mixture in any human being called upon by his country to belatedly face up to obvious despotism, previously long ignored. It is an image frozen stiff and still in the heat of battle, by God's camera at the lousy face of war.

His eyes are still open. His sighting eye is still squinting through the rear gun sight, looking directly at me, but not seeing me... through a ghastly faint glaze that has crept across each cornea. It is as once a mystery and a contradiction. But then I see it... a small hole just above his sighting eye, marring the otherwise clean features on a brave, stoic face.

With even more apprehension I move slowly around, directly to the side of Bob and his BAR. His helmet is still in place, and he is still in the firing position he held the night before. His body is braced and buttressed in his hole against the terrific inertia of the incoming, on-aimed round. The small hole in his forehead comes out big in the back of his head. It must have been a single, spent round, among the millions of tracers filling the sky last night, that perchance took this deadly pathway.

War is, and always be through eternity an absolute, unmitigated, immoral, ghastly hell... but the loss of freedom is far worse. No one, absolutely no one has to tell this to anyone of the small group of teenage GI witnesses assembled here. They stand with boundless respect and silent prayer this miserable, frozen grey morning on the Alsatian plateau by the Rhine, this 29 Nov. 1944.

The unvarnished face of war. The explicit truth and unlimited shock of the image before us easily sinks in, as the extent of the damage to this young man becomes apparent to all of us. Considerable quantities of white brain material had blown out a huge exit hole in the back of his head, sprayed and deflected off the back inside of his helmet, and then ricocheted and splattered down over the entire receiver and stock end of his BAR.

It covered his right hand and trigger finger… still on the trigger… still firing at the enemy flashes on the far side of that God forsaken pasture. In short, that round had blown the boy's brains out. What else is there to say?

With a second reflex action I turn slowly to Don Weiskopff and say: "My God, he was firing the instant that round hit!"

Weiskopff comes back: "Yup, that's what he was doing all right!"

Mexico, Slotnick, Weiskopff and I have to turn away from this scene and join the column for another day. We had learned that we couldn't stand by and ponder such things for very long and maintain sanity of any sort. But we also knew what would happen because we had seen it too many times.

Within a day or so, usually after the lifeless body was stiff from rigor mortis, it would be picked up by graves registration squads, tossed into the back of an open ¾ ton truck with all of the other KIAs of the day. With stiff arms and legs interlocking grotesquely, randomly stacked, they looked like a damnable pile of cord wood. This gruesome load would be trucked off to a central collection depot. So much for the body stacks and body counts of WW2.

So it is that Pete, Mexico, Slotnick, Weiskopff, Ballentine, Sgt. Cone and I… and all the rest of the 315th Infantry, together move out into about forty more rising suns and bitter cold dawns, for me ending on 15 January 1945. Mexico had two wars to fight… one for the USA, one for Mexico. Slotnick also had two wars to fight… one for the USA, one for Poland.

The world is indeed getting smaller… even in 1944, surely by mega factors in the 21st Century. In about 17 days, only 75 miles to the north of us, young American teenagers of Easy Co., Band of Brothers, will be put to the test in the Battle of the Bulge, North. They would reply with the historic "Nuts" to a Nazi surrender ultimatum.

Chapter Nine - Part E
Combat chow; on the front lines in the ETO "Chowhound -101" for all GI's everywhere in WW2

There is not much a "line troop" Dog Face infantryman will not do when it comes to satisfying his eternally insatiable appetite. All GIs are Chowhounds, including those dog faces of Bill Mauldin cartoon fame, we have all written the script for this sophisticated course: Chowhounds 101. Listen and learn …it may come in handy someday.

This soldier correspondent is thoroughly convinced that subsistence on the US Field Ration "K" for any length of time at all is enough, in itself, to drive any soul to desperate measures. He will go out on a combat patrol packin' BARs, M-1 Rifles, and Tommy guns plus M-300 field radios looking for Jerries and come back with two buck deer.

He will plead for a requisition, appropriate, buy, beg, or purloin from the local ''Frenchy" (local townsfolk of Alsace villages) anything edible he may possess, in any form. More than likely, Frenchy's edible creatures may include anything from a bedraggled wet goose, duck, pigeon, or rabbit, to 'porky' the pig or even genuine beef. Within five minutes after he is billeted in a particular town, he knows the exact coordinates of every single hen nest in the area, along with the time Frenchy makes his egg collecting rounds.

Having secured all the 'makins' for his meal, he will persevere in skinning, cooking or frying over anything hot… then adding a touch of French-fries or hash browns. All of this is of course is delicately seasoned with 'bouillon' powder from his K Ration, supper unit. Subsequently, the meal is usually devoured in five minutes flat. Like I said, he is both an author and a graduate of Chowhound 101.

This soldier correspondent, being the only Deutsch speaking GI in our platoon, handles the business end of most of these deals. Notice I have been very careful to avoid the word 'steal'… to do so would slander the character of our ranks. This kind of action is seldom taken, and then, only when the locals prove mean and hostile… hardly ever the case.

We have a lot of bartering and swapping power. Primarily: US Field Ration "K" (D-bar) Hard dark chocolate bars; "C" Ration meat units; "K" Ration candy and cigarettes. There is no barter guide for what Frenchy would offer us in return. Occasionally an extra D-bar would be requested.

Consider this: A D-bar; Mini-pack of cigarettes, and a C-Ration can of eat and Vegetable Stew would bring a nice, plump, fat chicken or rabbit and perhaps a bonus! Again, driven onward by the horrible apparition of a cold K-Ration can of 'Corned Pork Loaf,' our resourceful Dog Face GI becomes very adept at preparing meals.

Grease for frying is usually obtained from the bacon cans out of our friendly Tank Destroyer units "Ten in One" field rations. These guys always have bacon grease to spare, and we don't much worry about fat intake in WW2. We fry the chickens, boil and then fry rabbits, we cut the potatoes into sticks, then fry them in small batches in very hot grease, and drain them well! This, to match real home cooking.

Next: To understand the flexibilities of our Dog Face culinary arts we must first examine our WW2 Field Ration Complex.

Exact Contents of our field K-Rations (Cans in all units, flat cylindrical, opened with a key):

[B] Unit (Breakfast): 1 Can of either chopped pork and egg yolks" (lousy) or "Chopped Ham and Eggs (darn good); 4 dog biscuit crackers, 2½" square, hard enough to break our teeth; 1 Fruit Bar (dried fruits prunes, raisins and figs pressed into a dense bar lx ½ x 3"; (1) packet of powdered coffee; 2-3 lumps of sugar; 1 packet of 4 cigarettes; and 1 stick of gum. [D] Unit (Dinner/Lunch): (1) Can of processed American Cheese; (4) dog biscuits; (1) box of candy caramel; (1) packet of synthetic lemon or orange powder; plus sugar, cigarettes and gum. [S] Unit (Supper-Evening): (1) can of "Corned Pork Loaf" or "Beef and Pork Loaf" (this soldier has seen both of these turned down by a starving French poodle!); (4) dog biscuits; (1) bar of hard but sweet chocolate, sized as the fruit bar; (1) packet of bouillon soup powder (this is too salty to drink, we use it as a neat salt/pepper/spice seasoning to make the 'loaf' edible… how about that!) plus sugar, cigarettes and gum. There you have your chance to enhance culinary creativity! Let's get hot.

"Ten in One" Rations are issued to Tank & TD Bos., Artillery guys, & rear-echelon, but never to line infantry. Bummer, boo-hiss. These rations are packed in a large 12x18x24" box, enough for 10 guys while providing more flexibility and variety. The food is in larger cans: bacon, wax beans, jam, un-melted butter, yes and dog biscuits, tasting more like "Graham Crackers." Clear discrimination here at best or, at worst, a sinister plot against the infantry.

Now back to Chowhound 101 Creativity. With a potato bin in every cellar, we dice them into 3/8" cubes, mix them in a frying pan with K Ration B-Unit ham and eggs and a little grease, and fry the mix crispy brown. We cook the fruit bars in a little water, stir into a nice jam and smother it on our arf-arf biscuits. Turns out this soldier is the only soul in the ETO who does not mix up and drink his coffee-packet. Hence all the boys in my squad are always showering me with chocolate and fruit bars in trade for my coffee-packet. Confoozin' but Amoozin'!

The K-Ration D-Unit can of cheese is easily split in half with the key strip. We slice in half the cylindrical contents in two parts, heat it into a creamy-sticky state. Then we toast a plate full of dog biscuits, impregnate same with melted butter, spread on the melted cheese. Then we broil the platter upside down over an open fire.

The [D] Unit (Dinner/Lunch) lemonade and orange powder now need some attention.

The lemonade, universally hated, is too sour, too short on sugar. We mix the orange aid over strength with extra sugar, add crushed ice and we have a delight similar to a "World's Fair" class, double strength, cold "Orange Crush" Or it is like a specialty tea when hot.

The [S] Unit (Supper) is another matter… very difficult to do anything with. Some GI's grab the chocolate bar and throw the rest away. The diced spud addition does make the pork-loaf a little less horrible. There are inadvertent instances of "bad endings" which can befall any creative culinary Dog Face. A concerted effort to produce some mouthwatering hot cakes ends in absolute disaster when our "flour" turns out to be "Plaster of Paris." Heck, who can read these dang German labels anyway? End of story at least we tried.

What about the Company kitchen jeeps that come through like angels on Thanksgiving, Christmas and New Year's? Well when we are on the move and in the attack mode, the kitchen staff is too far behind the lines. If we are lucky enough to stay billeted in one town for four days, they do get some hot meals up to us. Their "hot-cake" breakfasts are really something else… things we all dream and long for. These do help a tad to mitigate disasters like the sad one above.

So, we end this session of Chowhound 101.

Chapter Nine - Part F
Schweighausen, Ohlungen, and Winterhausen regimental picture

29 Nov. After the capture of Batzendorf in the morning, the 1st Battalion moves to the South Moder Sector just to the NW. Charlie Co. closes in on Winterhausen at 1000.

30 Nov. Abel Company is motorized to Uhlwiller at 0945 hours. The 1st Battalion CP moves to Ohlungen at 1800. The 2nd Battalion discovers a group of Germans and two tanks near its area, clearing it out with slight resistance.

Later a patrol followed by the bulk of the Battalion advance on Ohlungen, receiving a lot of fire mortar and flat trajectory fire. Entry into the town itself is made easily while the enemy continued to defend the northern section. These are eliminated and many prisoners taken.

Meanwhile Early in the morning the 3rd Battalion occupies Uhlwiller unopposed.

An AT gun and a 15-man German patrol flanking attack are encountered and dispatched. All told, the Regiment took 62 prisoners. Their approach at the outskirts of Schweighouse is a different matter. This requires very heavy fighting until the town is finally cleared in spite of two blown bridges.

Regimental picture

On 1 Dec. Baker and Dog Cos. move to Uhlwiller on 1-3 December. The 2nd Battalion advances to Wintershausen, and the 3rd Battalion heads towards Uhlwiller. The Stage is now set for a complex battle for this bitterly contested South Moder area.

It is to involve night patrols across the Moder along with the usual machine gun mayhem and the thunder of artillery and mortars, real big ones…50% larger than the 81mm mortars standard in our heavy weapons companies, D, H, and M.

The Big Blue 79 has established a key roadblock north of the Moder River. This is the side the Germans think is theirs, deluded souls) just west of Schweighouse. The slightest eyewink or twitch of anyone in this roadblock had been evoking instant Kraut fire from one of these monster 120mm tubes ((4.7" the size of 5" Naval guns) from their "void-pocket" position near Schweighausen. Bad News. But fortunately, the bums vacated the position last night.

Today our 2nd and 3rd Battalions clean up their respective sections of Schweighausen of hold out Germans. The prisoner count for the day is 16. This brings the cumulative 315 prisoner count since D-Day to 6962. That is almost a half of a German Div. taken out of action!!

2 Dec: Early in the morning our 3rd Bo. sends out a combat patrol across the river to the factory area north of Schweighausen, they encounter a heavy volume of MG (machine gun) fire and are ordered to withdraw. Patrols indicate no enemy contact east of the factory area but do spot some assault guns and tanks.

Our 1st Battalion sends out patrols with no enemy contact. Late in the day a strong combat patrol, supported by our 9041h FA, crosses the river successfully at a spot where our I&R Platoon failed to do so previously. Under this determined American assault the enemy broke rapidly. Thereafter, a 3000-yard stretch of the river is clear for our patrol crossings.

Our objective is to establish a bridgehead on the north side of the Moder. During the night I&R and Recon troops attempt but fail to establish a bridgehead (to facilitate passage of a 1st Battalion Patrol). They draw a hail of misery from the enemy including mortars, small arms and Burp Gun fire.

3 Dec: Enemy fire in Schweighausen sector starts the day with a vengeance. This is their last stand in the defense of NE France, *and it shows.* They throw everything they have at us including their delight-ful 120mm mortars along with barrages of 20 and 50mm (0.78 & 2") automatic AA cannon fire. A 1st Battalion combat patrol including four men from the I&R Platoon cross the river and reach the railroad without trouble.

They find one bridge blown in this locality and one-foot bridge intact. In the Regimental area two enemy planes were spotted, and one is shot down. A portable shower unit is now installed and a rec. room is set up for the troops. In the new home of an ex-Nazi with radio, record player and writing facilities. Shades of civilization!

4 Dec: Enemy fire in the Schweighausen sector is notably diminished and a 2nd Battalion patrol found very little activity, while other patrols draw some MG fire.

5 – 6 Dec: Two quiet days. A new Corps assignment now puts the 79th Division in close association with the 45th and 103rd Infantry Divisions along with 14th Armored Division. Regimental patrol patterns continue with little change.

7 Dec: In their last fling south of the Moder River the enemy poured in 100 rounds of combined fire, again 120mm mortars plus 100-lS0mm artillery. 315th moves from Ohlungen to Weitbruch. 1st Battalion departs by foot at 1400- closes in at 1800.

Chapter Nine - Part G
Out of foxholes and into warm billets. This soldier correspondent interpreting with limited high school German.

We GI Dog Faces often complain bitterly about long foot marches, but there are occasions in which the Reg. CO decides it is more cost effective, or battle objectives time essential, to put us on 2½ trucks for the ride.

On these occasions Billeting Parties are required and don't work at the Regimental level. For very practical reasons it must be handled by Platoon level Billeting Parties.

Enter the Baker Company 2nd Platoon generic model for any Billeting Party in operation, anywhere in Lorraine or Alsace.

It is 1800 hours as we close in on this good sized, typical Alsatian village anywhere on the Liberation Battle Route. The dark, shadowy form of an endless motor convoy can barely be seen halted along a winding cobblestone street of the town. The chill of winter is in the air as the GI's of B Co., 315th Reg., poke free of overcoats, gather their equipment and vault off the trucks.

The 1st Battalion Commander has given our CO a specific sector of town in which to billet his troops. The order is passed down. and off in the dark somewhere I hear the voice of T/Sgt. Bob Nixon, our acting Platoon Leader, assembling the 2nd Platoon. [This an officer's job and Nixon has turned it down 5 times.] There has been no advanced billeting party, so as usual in cases like this... "Westy" (as the guys call this soldier correspondent) is called up front to operate with the 2nd Platoon CP Billeting Party as translator and negotiator. It seems this soldier correspondent is the only guy in the Platoon who knows any German at all, even though at a limited, 2-year high school level.

This qualification along with a bunch of practical experience over the past several weeks... *nails me for the job.*

We have to talk Frenchy out of a house... a place to sleep and get warm, for about 38 GI's...no small task. Unlike with the hated Nazi behavior, we choose to operate in a spirited negotiation mode with a *very delicate balance.* We don't just commandeer, and so the stage is set the story that follows, typical of that in all Alsatian villages.

We enter through a rusty old gate into the inner court (or barnyard) of the dwelling, follow a wrought iron rail up the steps to a heavy, foreboding, blacked outdoors. We bang heavily on the only available window. After some time, a faint flicker of lamp light can be seen through a tiny crack. An old peasant woman tentatively opens the door. She is all decked out, complete with night gown. She draws back, in obvious surprise, frightened no doubt by the wicked looking ¾ inch flash-hider on my BAR automatic rifle. It really does make the weapon look like a 20mm cannon, though it was clearly pointed at the ground.

The lessons I learned to date on this Billeting job are to be very clear about handling civilians understandably distraught. One must be polite and courteous, yet unyielding and firm. Above all, *never get involved in an argument.* They will out-talk you every time.

As we move in, I try to be as low key as possible, explaining not to be alarmed. We want only a place to get warm and sleep for the night. I stay away from mentioning the 38-man size of our Platoon, focusing instead on the 12-man squad by squad. This is until we ascertain how many she has room to sleep on the floor.

She leads us into what apparently is her only room...a living-dining room combination. Now I can quickly size up the troop capacity of this floor, while also easily spotting the door to her only bedroom *which we never touch.* I also inquire about the kitchen which is as yet mentioned. Must have thought we were crazy to want to sleep on the kitchen floor!

Satisfied that she had enough room for at least 24 GI's, I move a couple of squads in. This gentle old lady was excited and distraught by the whole thing. She stayed up all the rest of the night. Keep in mind that the great majority (perhaps 90%) of these French-Alsace folks are very friendly, hate the Bosche bitterly and fear them worse. There are a few very mean and uncooperative, but hardly a basis for an overall judgment.

Chapter Nine - Part H
Uhlwiller Western Outpost of the South Moder billeting party. The Saga of the dud German shell!

The entire South Moder Sector, west of Haguenau, where this action takes place is small, about 2 ½ x S miles. This is the size of central Wyoming Ohio, the action time frame is just one week, (1- 7 December 1944), but what an amazing story this week tells about the 2nd Platoon of Baker Company, reported here by this soldier correspondent, BAR man, 2nd Squad. Uniquely the nature of the battle here does not require foxholes.

It does however require continuous combat patrols under a nightmare umbrella of thundering, cross firing artillery and mortars. The good news is that we will be billeting troops in warm houses for a change.

But, bummer... the bad news is that billeting is far from easy to accomplish as witnessed by the dramatic tale below. The Reg. CP is in Ohlungen during the entire week.

This saga is indeed a heartwarming vignette of human interaction at the face of war. It turns out to be quite a drama, with two Paul Harvey style "Rest of the Story" footnotes.

The day of Saturday 2 December breaks cold and nippy for all GI's in the Platoon. The MO (method of op) is that of the Generic, Platoon Billeting Party.

As described above. This is followed as a pattern, below.

To his dismay, this soldier correspondent becomes involved in billeting the western most outpost of the Regiment, crucial to 79th Div. military objectives. Under military orders our 3rd Platoon had just taken over a house to be used as an OP (observation post). The intelligence our OP saves the lives of GI's. Our 1st Platoon is now ordered into the same house as replacements.

Now the fun begins. We have nine men including this soldier correspondent and need the large front room to sleep in. I approach the lady of the house with the standard billeting request. This 'bedraggled' old woman is simply wretched... a product of this dang war!

All during the most recent 21 days, the war had really been brought home to her. She and her family had been forced to live in the cellar by heavy artillery shelling. As our Billeting negotiations now proceed, the artillery has apparently ceased, and she now wants to live in the large front room. Hence, she proceeds to unburden her entire life's troubles on me. She then becomes emotionally shaken and rambles on for some time. My little bit of German often gets me in trouble. In spite of my slow, halting spoken German, she vastly overestimates the speed at which I can comprehend. But it is obvious to me that... she has nine kids and cannot possibly fit them all into her small back room.

Perhaps our Platoon should move our OP to her neighbor's house...they have less kids. This all winds up in an emotional crescendo with half of the family present. Then, heaven help us all, she starts to cry. This is the living end for me! They never taught us how to handle situations like this back at Fort Benning Basic. This soldier takes a deep breath and seriously contemplates turning in his 746 MOS - BAR man for something else... don't know what. Un-possessed of any Nazi characteristics we are totally hog tied. We had already explained that we were under military orders... to no avail.

So here we have a bunch of rough tough fightin' men, who kill by the numbers, held at bay because, above all, we are human American kids. My mistake was giving her an inch... reason to believe she might debate the situation. In the end we merely started cleaning up the mess in the room and refused to talk any further. She gets the idea.

There is a "Paul Harvey, The Rest of the Story" at play here. There is a small ante-room connected to the large front room. It has a bed but no stove. It is sized to sleep all GI's in the one big room. The old lady had definitely planned to use this room as well.

At 0200 hours in the black dead of night, one, single, German, dud artillery shell comes screaming out of the night. With a thunderous shock, it crashes through the roof of our CP house, and rips right through the bed in that small back room. This is exactly where she would have been sleeping had she won the argument. It finds its final resting place lodged in a basement beam.

It shook all hell loose and left the room in a mess. It is hard to describe the sheer power and staccato concussive sound a dud, 105 mm, dud artillery shell makes hitting a house like a sledgehammer yet without exploding. It has the shock and awe of a bolt of lightning or a meteorite rock screaming out to the sky. Believe me, it shakes up, to the core, every living soul in our CP house. Enough said. Both the Americans and the Alsatians are winners.

Chapter Nine - Part I
Weitbruch... our last battle sector south of Haguenau and the Moder River. 7-mile foot march, Uhlwiller to Weitbruch...

Our 1st Battalion departs Uhlwiller by foot at 1400 and closes in on Weitbruch at 1800, to positions formerly occupied by the 313th Regiment of the Big Blue 79. This is another small battle town about 51/251/2 miles SE of South Moder Sector just departed. Key villages included are: Weitbruch, Niederscbaffolsheim, Marienthal and Bischwiller, all south of the Moder River and Oberhoffen just to the north of the river.

The 2nd Battalion moves to Niederschaffolsheim, to be on standby in reserve, ready to assist the 1st and 3rd attacking Bos. The 6th Corps attack objective is Kaltenhaus. It is to be an enormous attack by three full American Divisions (45,000 men, an overwhelming power density packed into a tiny 25 sq. miles.) with the goal to drive the Nazi Wehrmacht clean-up to the NE corner of France, and back to the Siegfried line north of the Lauter River.

The deployment Plan: 45th Div. on the left; 103rd Div. in the center; 94th Cavalry Recon Squadron patrolling the right flank. The Big Blue 79 is to be deployed; 314th on the left; 315th in the center; and the 3131 on the right. The 79th mission is to capture Seltz to the NE. The Regimental missions are: 315th to seize Marientbal and Kaltenhaus, assist the 314th in taking Haguenau, and then to the north, Soufflenheim and Seltz. Meanwhile, the 14th Armored is to be prepared to pass through the 103rd Div. and head for the Siegfried Line.

Our 1st Battalion mission: Contain enemy locations to its front; send one company with the rest of the Battalion establish roadblocks; destroy trapped enemy, and assist the 3rd Battalion in liberating Marienthal.

Chapter Nine - Part J
The equipment, weapons and ordinance upon which the combat GI's life depends Dateline: 11 Nov.1944 -15 Jan. 1945, Alsace-Lorraine

Overview: There are a hundred ways for a GI to wind up listed on the Morning Report as WIA, KIA, MIA (wounded, killed or missing in action). All are bad news.

Aside from bad training and battle tactics, the keyways are bad equipment and bad weapons and bad ordinance (the bullets, shells, explosive warheads propelled by the guns). Another equal opportunity category of ways to get killed or sent back is with incapacitating trench foot, frostbite, includes bad clothing, capes, camouflage, socks, boots and gear.

In this second category, for example, this soldier correspondent may not have been seen or hit by the white caped German Sniper... if I too had a white cape. The flip side. I didn't, and I got hit. I could have had a far worse fate 2 days later on 1/17. I could have been killed or captured along with my assistant BAR man. Clearly it is a no-win situation. For now, the subject is equipment, weapons and ordnance.

It has been said that the American Army was the best equipped in the world in WW2. In my view is that it is true quantitatively, but qualitatively... not *always*. The totally out-gunned American Sherman tank is a case in point. So is the case of the 1918 Pom-Pom gun BAR versus the German Burp Gun for the hip shooting kind of fighting we did in WW2. Our USA military gun and ordnance engineers and "pentagon" brass have the human nature tendency to get stuck in old habits and attitudes. The sickening airpower versus the battleship snit of the 1920's comes to mind. So does this same malady impact development in all categories.

But wow! Today we can all take comfort in the enormous strides current military has *made* in weapons development all the way from the fabulous M-16 AR to the M-1 Abrams Tank.

Back to 1944. I want to present a comparative picture of the issues that count most to the GI Dog Face Infantry of the line ID, and to their comrades in the airborne, paratroop, and marines. When the rubber hits the road, these are the guys that make that wiggly black line on the map, move back and forth. The general conception is that we shine primarily in small arms, while the German forte is in extremely high muzzle velocity, very flat trajectory guns typified by their versatile 88mm gun

Our crowning glory is the semi-automatic M-1 rifle, in its time, the best rifle in the world, no contest. I cite an incident case in point. The M-1, because of its fast semi-automatic, 4-5 rounds per second firing rate, saves the life of a man in our 1st Platoon. It is during house-to-house fighting. A BAR man is getting ready to fire around the cover of a brick wall, when abruptly a Jerrie steps out of a doorway takes aim on the BAR man *from the left rear.*

Get this picture now. Still further behind these two another GI had been popping off at a good rate on a German sniper with his M-1. He is just ready to squeeze off another round when he catches an instantaneous glance of the Jerry, at this second lining up his sights on our BAR man. By reflex action the GI whirls and, not having time to aim, sends a hip fired round zinging past Jerry's head. It didn't hit him, but the second shot did… My case for the M-1 rests. One more targeted BAR man is saved.

In fully automatic weapons overall the Jerries have the edge on us! We have only four, 30 cal. automatics, the BAR, the light and heavy MG, and the Thompson 45 cal. sub-machine gun. The Jerries have a whole slew of "Burp Guns" so named because their cyclic rate of fire is so incredibly fast the individual shots cannot be distinguished.

I have carried the BAR for most of my combat days and can speak objectively pro and con. It is made almost entirely of heavy machined parts is precisely why the dang thing weighs 20 lbs instead of the needed 10 to 12 lbs.

Used with a bi-pod which can be seen on countless war videos, swinging crazily around the muzzle while carried on the march. It can pick off the enemy accurately at 1000 yards. I call it my "Pom-Pom" gun because of its low firing rate of 240 rounds/min (an intimidating rounds per second.) It will pin down Jerries, and cover movements. In many cases bring them out of stubborn defenses hollering "kamerad."

Chapter Nine - Part K
Kaltenhaus, 6th Corps objective with 3 Divisions
Dateline: Sat. 9 Dec.44. - Attack towards Marienthal and Kaltenhaus begins

During the night preceding the attack, the enemy is comparatively quiet. As the attack jumps off at 0715 our 1st Battalion encounters numerous, well prepared log bunkers with superb fields of crossfire, heavy mortar and artillery fire along with flat trajectory 88mm assault guns. The progress is slow but inflicts heavy casualties on the enemy.

The 2nd Battalion is committed at noon and by night fall still remains in contact with the enemy. The 3rd Battalion jumps off and reduces a strong point under heavy mortar and small arms fire. It reaches the southern fringe of Marienthal and clears this with little difficulty. However, they get stopped by heavy fire of all kinds including two 88mm assault guns and possibly tanks. They are still in contact in the darkness.

On our right the 313th makes a rapid advance, liberating Bischwiller and taking 135 prisoners. On our left the 314th is having a heck of a time with very stiff resistance in Haguenau. Our 315th takes 25 prisoners during the day while suffering light casualties.

Dateline: **Sun 10 Dec. 1944 - Attack on Kaltenhaus resumes.**

Attack jumps off again. Early in the morning the 2nd Battalion attacking Marienthal is able to enter the town with no opposition and taking 7 prisoners. Later in the day they encounter problems at the Moder River, wide and deep with blown bridges in the vicinity of Oberhoffen north of the river. This forces the 2nd Battalion to make a wide detour to attack Camp Oberhoffen.

They reach as far as the SW edge of the airport in the vicinity of the town. It is in the early morning darkness that the 3rd Battalion sends a reinforced platoon into Marienthal, only to find that the Germans have evacuated leaving only a six-man rear guard. Later on, in the afternoon, they are forced to make the same detour as did the 2nd Battalion, to get across the river, heading for an attack on Oberhoffen and then Schirrhein 5 mi. north of the river.

Incredibly, it is our 1st Battalion that takes one VI Corps objective, Kaltenhouse. Having received harassing fire during the night, the attack is launched at 1200. The Battalion gets great supporting fire from tanks and TD's and is able to cross the area with considerable speed. Just prior to entry some MG fire is encountered, but the town is cleared quickly by 1630, taking 29 prisoners. We do get more intense artillery harassing fire from 2100-2150. The Regimental prisoner total for the day is 52 with exceedingly light casualties for the ground covered. The 3rd Battalion follows the 2nd Battalion in making the wide detour in route to attack between Oberhoffen and Schirrheim and Camp Oberhoffen.

Chapter Nine - Part L
Camp d'Oberhoffen big surprise for 315th GIs

Dateline: **Sun.10 Dec.1944 - The spitting image of Camp Forest, TN**

Lise Pommois has a delightful introduction to Camp Oberhoffen in her book, Winter Storm, very appropriate to insert here: "GI's Capture Home Camp."

"Members of the 315th Infantry who drink Oberhoffen Lager (beer) rub their eyes and look twice when they come to Camp d'Oberhoffen, a Kraut Basic Training Center. Until they notice the German lettered signs in the area, they think they have stumbled on a European replica of Camp Forrest, Tennessee, where the 79th underwent maneuvers.

Neatly arranged barracks dot the garrison area and officers' quarters reveal an array of highly polished, overstuffed furniture resting on polished floors. The area beyond the garrison proper is broken up into a variety of rifle ranges, complete with targets. Human silhouettes depicting the Nazi version of the American soldier, reveal a paunchy, sad-sack type of GI dragging an overstuffed musket at trail-arms.

Three prisoners, taken in the area, said the Germans had built Oberhoffen as a refresher camp for seasoned soldiers. Recently, however, as the war moved closer to the Reich, it has been used as a basic training and finishing school. Until a few days ago, these men were essential railroad workers in Germany, exempt from the draft.

With no preliminaries, they were ordered into uniforms and given two days of training with 88's, featured by firing four practice rounds. Then, taken to Oberhoffen, they were handed rifles and ordered to fight as infantry replacements. One of them, obviously speaking for the three, remarked plaintively 'I don't see how Hitler can win a war with soldiers like us.'"

The thing that catches the eye of this soldier correspondent in the segment above is "huge modern kitchen." Obviously, a prime target for a Chowhound 101 recon squad. I was there and remember it well after 63 years in close association with an energetic Chowhound patrol from Baker Co., so now hear this.

We are the ones who were duped into the "Plaster of Paris" hot-cake fiasco by conniving culprits. Clearly, some mischievous misfits (could be rear guard Germans), but more likely it was ill-advised GI's from our own 2nd Battalion who loaded this attractive "box of flour" in amongst all the *genuine cooking supplies* in the Camp Oberhoffen kitchen cabinets. A booby trap, pure and simple. Bummer. Someday their conscience will do them in!

Liberation of Camp Oberhoffen; Sunday 10 Dec.1944
The 2nd Battalion attacks and occupies Camp Oberhoffen, supported by the 1st Battalion and TD's. The Regimental CP is established in the town of Oberhoffen.

Liberation of Haguenau; Mon.11 Dec.1944.
Haguenau, a key rail and communications center, is taken by the 314th striking hard and fast. Evidence is the Germans suffer severe losses and casualties necessitating a hasty retreat. Throughout the night

and early morning hours they pound the 314th with harassing mortar, 75mm-150mm fire. By 0700 most of the enemy withdraws towards Wissembourg.

Chapter Nine - Part M
Dateline: Tues 12 Dec 1944, Just North of the Moder River

Our 1st Battalion departs Oberhoffen at 1300 by foot north bound for Schirrhein, closing in at 1600, after a patrol had confirmed enemy withdrawal. The 3rd Battalion followed, occupying Schirrhoffen. All highways north to the Siegfried Line are jammed all day with troops and vehicles of other units, delaying our advance.

The 313th spearheaded the chase on the right flank, pushing rapidly up the Rhine valley, followed by the 315th• The objective of the Big Blue 79 is to stay in contact with the enemy at all times, and thus prevent them from getting back to man the Siegfried defenses. But no soap. The Krauts manage their retreat very skillfully, blowing bridges and causing rearguard mayhem to slow us down.

Chapter Nine – Part N
Niederroedern and Eberbach-Zeltz, Niederlauterbach,
Scheibenhard and Neuwiller, first into Germany
Dateline: Wed. 13 Dec 1944

The 315th spends most of the day awaiting the replacement of a blown bridge at Niederroedern. At 0730 our 1st Battalion moves out of the woods towards Niederroedern, but the attack is delayed until early afternoon, clearing the town at about 1300. From there they jump off to liberate Eberbach-Zeltz, 2 miles to the north, at 1500.

Niederlauterbach, Scheibenhard and Neuwiller
Dateline: Thurs 14 Dec 1944

At 0930 the 315th moves out in Battalion column formation with the 2nd Battalion leading to liberate the Niederlauterbach- Scheibenhard area. Resistance is light until the Lauter River is approached, evoking 88mm, plus small arms and MG crossfire. Proceeding 2 miles SE to Neuwiller the increasing intensity of the crossfire pins down some elements.

During the day 41 prisoners are taken and a German defense map is captured indicating our enemy opposition is the 476th Regiment. 1st Battalion patrols indicate that Niederlauterbach is occupied in force. They then order six battalions of our FA (Field Artillery) to pound the town. At 0630 we attack the town in strength and are able to get in before the defenders could be warned. The town is easily captured, and 31 prisoners are taken including an entire MG platoon.

First into Germany Dateline: Fri 15 Dec 1944

It is a historic day when the 315th puts the first man across the Lauter River border into Germany in WW2. During the black night and early morning, the 2nd Battalion enters the town of Scheibenhard, France, with two companies. This is a historic, two-part town, north and south, divided by the Lauter. Just north across the Lauter is Germany.

After daylight begins a slow, bitter battle, house to house cleanup. By 1800 hours the south town is cleared, but the north town is still bitterly contested, defended by the whole bit (small arms, MG's, mortars, 88's, and heavy artillery). The 2nd Battalion Fox Company sends a man across the footbridge. S/Sgt. Dewey J. White, of Miller, Ohio, has the honor of being the first guy in the entire Allied Army to set foot into Germany.

Also, Sgt. White is the soldier farthest east and deepest into Germany on the Western Front. With entrenched enemy we cannot exploit the foot bridge. 50 prisoners are taken. All of the north and south towns are captured the next day. The 315th goes defensive.

CHAPTER TEN

Chapter Ten – Part A

PREFACE REMARKS: The action timeline for this chapter covers the period 16 December through 1 January 1945. The primary source documents are war letters written 63 years ago. WW2 is raging everywhere. It is 6 months after D-Day Normandy.

D'Jeanne of 'Die Lorelei'. Billeting Saga in Neuwiller

A tranquil interlude punctuating the death and destruction in the war to liberate Alsace. This story tugs at the heartstrings of humanity, Americans, and of Alsatians alike. It serves as a stark reminder of just how small our world is, and of the unquenchable warmth and sensitivity of the human spirit... all amidst the sheer horror, thunder and gripping fear induced at the convoluted face of war.

Chapter Ten - Part B
First entry - getting acquainted (the story of singing Die Loralie together)
Dateline: Sat. 16 Dec.1944

For this soldier correspondent this is to be the last, and most memorable billeting party of the war.

During Thursday and Friday combat and patrol events take us back and forth in the vicinity of Niederlauterbach and Neuwiller several times until both towns are cleared. However, for billeting purposes our 1st. Battalion leaves Niederlauterbach late Friday afternoon on the 2-mile foot march to Neuwiller, closing in at 1930.

In Baker Company, we split up in small groups and each squad becomes its own Billeting Party. We find the perfect small billet in a small house on the main drag of Neuwiller. It has room for only three of us in the 2nd Squad, but this turns out to be the perfect solution for both the Americans and Alsatians alike.

The following 4 days, 16 -19 December, we are heavily involved in patrolling and fighting in the Scheibenhardt vicinity and north. Of these, we are to stay billeted at least 3 days with this family in Neuwiller, before moving north to Scheibenhardt billets.

Here is the remarkable saga of d' Jeanne of 'Die Lorelei' presented in third person, starting out just as this soldier enters this small Alsatian home, 1700, 16 December.

Entering their home, a few elementary subsistence words of German come out of the young American's mouth, in an initial effort at communication. The impact on the farmer, his wife and daughter (Poppa, Ma, and d'Jeanne... sounding like Joan) is almost electric.

They are not altogether sure this that this fuzzy faced American kid had ever shaved yet, much less had time to learn German, anywhere. Mystified, they learn about a man named 'Shadrack' (Herr Shaterian, H.S. German teacher) in eine Amerikanisch Hochschule, in der kleine dorf Westfield, New Jersey, USA.

Totally starved for communication with Americans they proceed to pour out their souls to the young GI at verbal fire rate, doubtful that even Shadrack could receive. With heartfelt feeling and patience, the young American has to slow them down a little, keeping them to the basics. But communicate they do!

With the warmest hospitality they invite their young GI guests to share what little dinner they have, and even offer their quaint 'in-the-wall' beds for what remains of the dark night. Both are politely declined. With an urgent top priority, the dog-tired GI's sleep on the floor.

The next day, Sunday 17 December, this war-torn group does share meals, GI 'K Rations' and lots of warm milk. During the day the reality of all of this takes a while to sink in for this Alsatian family. As evening approaches their curiosity just cannot be disguised or contained. The emotional level really starts to build up around the quiet lamp-lit dinner table.

The night settled in on this tiny group of humanity in an incredulous, 'Shangri-La' like, respite from the thunderous winds of war. They all dearly need the rest. The rays from the lamps seem to grow fainter as the subject turns to Folk Music.

The American asks if the family could sing 'Die Lorelei'? (A folk ballad, banned by Hitler, about a sailor on the Rhine River, and a siren, the Lorelei, perched up high above). The Alsatians' eyes light up like electronic flashes, far brighter than the lamps in the darkened room. This American lad has to be kidding! Do Americans know Stephen Foster, My Darling Clementine, or Red River Valley?

To the astonishment of the Alsatians the young GI writes down the six verses with very little help. And then, as God is my witness, slowly and deliberately in his rough, off- key voice, Poppa starts to sing out the melody and words of the first verse – "Ich weiss nicht was soil es bedeuten, Dass ich so traurig bin." (I know not what meaning is portended here… I am so sad and melancholy).

As the wiry young GI joins in, Ma, Pappa and d'Jeanne, already at their wits end, now simply cannot believe their ears. How can this be coming from this boy's mouth and heart? But now, with brightening faces that defy description they all join in with everything that is in their hearts and souls…their voices strong and clear, "Ein Märchen aus alten Zeiten, das kommt mir nicht aus dem Sinn." (A Tale of old times… it does not come back to me easily to mind).

The eyes of this war-ravaged family are now reflective and clearly moist. By this line it is tears that are running down those wonderful stoic faces, But they keep singing: "Die Luft ist kuhl, und es dunkelt, Und Ruhig fliesst der Rhein." (The air is cool, and it darkens, and peacefully, tranquilly flows the Rhein.)

By the fourth line, second verse, in an absolutely incredible scene at the face of war, the contagious tears finally join the young American soldier. He is now simply overwhelmed by the force of humanity at work, and by the sheer spontaneity of it all. But all four continue....

"Der Gipfel des Berges funkelt, Im abendsonnenschein." (The peaks of the mountains glisten, in the afternoon sunshine.)

They sing through the last four verses to the end of the ballad, and of this story. It is an interaction of two cultures, an ocean apart at just one of the millions of crossroads of WW2. Und das hat mit ihrem Singen, Die Lorelei getan. (I believe a big wave swamps the navigator on the river, putting an end to both ship and sailor; And this, she with her singing, the Lorelei hath done.)

Chapter Ten – Part C
Panic Among the Alsatian Civilians of NE France. News of Hitler's current Battle of the Bulge (Ardennes) offensive up north and of his forthcoming Operation Nordwind Reaches Civilians BEFORE Pfc. H. West
Dateline: **Mon. 18 December**

We are too busy trying to stay alive. Soldiers online are told only what they need to know. So it is that the morning after our Lorelei songfest by lamp light. I simply did not know of Hitler's ARDENNES Offensive {Battle of the Bulge, North, launched 16 Dec.).

However, in the wee hours of Monday 18 December, the morning just after we had just sang The Lorelei, this bad news surely does get to all the civilians in NE France. This is via an efficient grapevine, including the entire populace of Neuwiller and vicinity.

Our billet guard sees an old fellow and his family moving hastily down the street, south westward complete with all belongings in a baby carriage.

We know this means trouble. The Germans had made dire threats to all local towns they vacated, promising the unspeakable things they would do to the locals upon return. They leave a palpable cloud of fear and terror one could cut with a knife. By 0700 hours the whole town of Neuwiller was uneasy. We can sense this shifty unrest in Poppa, Ma, and Joan.

Later on, more and more loaded baby carriages go by, and finally a horse drawn wagon chuck full of family possessions. Joan drops her sewing and moves like lightening back and forth, window to door. That seems to settle it!

The whole family, all but Poppa who remains calm, scurry about collecting treasured possessions. Wooden shoes go in the corner and leather walking shoes come out of the closet. Clothes arc changed and a host of preparations are made for a fast journey.

I catch short glimpses of Ma's face as she hurries back and forth. The contrast with the night before is shocking. Sadly, it is racked in quivering horror. Branded into her features is a fear... a burning fear I have never seen before in the eyes of a human. She cries and sobs and is visibly trembling all over. It is a face I wish could be seen by millions of Americans!

It does no good to plead with Ma not to leave. The facts are on her side... and at the time this correspondent doesn't even know it. She only sobs more and runs her finger across her throat as she explains the Nazi Bosche had threatened and promised to come back and slit the throats of all civilians.

So it is that our dear "Lorelei" family departs the town Neuwiller this day, bound for points as far away from Hitler's Wehrmacht as they can get. Ma to Lord knows where, Joan to Paris? Poppa? He stays home to take care of the cows.

Chapter Ten – Part D
Big Blue 79 on the defensive; Momentous times in WW2 - ETO and Pacific
Dateline: 16 Dec.1944

This is not a day like any day, and this is not a month like any month. To say that these are indeed momentous times in WW2 is an understatement... We are at a turning point in the salvation of civilization.

In the ETO (European Theater of Operations) we are on the threshold of the coldest winter in memory or record. It is one with a landscape of solid frozen, solid white mountains filled with solid white caped, well trained, well equipped Nazi mountain troops. History books report that they "charge into battle" screaming, howling, & cursing louder than their own fire. Acting like they are drunk or doped! These insanely charging Germans are hollering "American Gangsters" and "Yankee bastards" at the top of their lungs. Real fun and games.

Chapter Ten – Part E
Historic timeline, Events in both the European & Pacific Theaters

December 1944 in Europe: 16-17 - Battle of the Bulge is starting in the Ardennes; 17 - Waffen SS murder 81 US POW's in Malmedy; 26 - Patton relieves Bastogne; 27 - Soviet troops besiege Budapest; 28 - Hitler hosts the final briefing on his plans for Operation Nordwind at Adersshorst-Giessen. (510) All Commanding Generals of Army Group 6 attend, including Von Rundstedt, Keitel, Himmler, and Jodi, etc.

The stage is set for the biggest battle of the Big Blue 79 in WW2 in Hatten and Rittershoffen. Pacific: 15 - US Troops invade Mindoro in the Philippines; 17 - US Air Force begins preps. to drop atomic bomb - establish 509th Composite Group, B-29's.

Then, January 1945 in Europe: 1-17 - Germans withdraw from the Ardennes, "The German High Command realizes the Ardennes offensive is bogged down, and Hitler wants to retain the initiative by launching a 2nd through." Battle of the Bulge- South, Operation Nordwind. 16 - US. 1st and 3rd armies link up after a month-long separation during the Battle of the Bulge (North); 17 - Soviet Troops take Warsaw; 26 - Soviet troops liberate Auschwitz!

Then, January 1945 in Pacific: 3 - Gen. MacArthur and Admiral Nimitz placed in command of all ground and naval forces for the attack on Okinawa and Japan itself.; 4 – British occupy Akyab in Burma; 9 - US 6th Army invades Lingayen Gulf, Luzon, Philippines; 11 - US. Carrier air raids on Jap bases in Indochina; 28 - The Burma Road is finally opened (it's closure by the Japs early in the war led to the formation of the famous Flying Tigers.

Chapter Ten - Part F
GI clothing, boots & gear
Dateline: **11 Nov 1944 -15 Jan 1945, Alsace- Lorraine**

We must add Incapacitated In Action (IIA) to the "hundred ways" the GI Dogface can wind up listed on the Co. Morning Report. All are bad - aside from bad equipment, weapons and ordnance, the crucial, equal opportunity category of ways to get sent back from the front is Incapacitation.

This can be of any part of the body required to move and to fight. Aside from disabling you as fighting soldier it can cripple one for life, so it deserves the same attention as weapons and ordnance.

It can send you back with trench foot, frostbite, or you-name-it. This includes the bad clothing, capes, camouflage, socks, boots and gear.

This is a life-threatening topic in two lousy fighting seasons: One, the cold, wet, rainy muddy fall, and two, the frozen, solid white winter.

The Cold, Wet, Rainy, Muddy Fall

Lise Pommois covers this topic well in her book Winter Storm (510), inserted here under the title: "Mud...Mud...Glorious Mud" and includes selected quotations from the men of the 45th Div. who had fought in Italy. It is comparable with 1944 fighting in muddy Lorraine.

The story starts off with a view of Alsace which sure matches Lorraine in the same season. The weather remained the same throughout the period; cloudy, cold, rain almost every day, visibility often poor. 'For the rain, it raineth every day" (Shakespeare). The foxholes were full of water before they had been dug out.

In Alsace Trench foot exacted its toll! The men from the 45th Inf. Division had experienced Italian mud in the previous winter. This time they were given better clothing: shoe-backs or overshoes, wool-lined parkas, combat suits and sleeping bags."

"A special effort was made to see each man should have a frequent change of socks. The men often made booties for their feet from old blankets. At night they had to take off their soggy socks, massage their feet, and wear booties while the shoes and socks were drying. GI's also discovered the insulating qualities of paper."

H West – "Hogwash! Not so for the Blue 79, Except for shoe packs...

This soldier never saw any of this stuff in Lorraine, and the question is why not?"

The Nov. 1944 experience of our 1st Battalion Lorraine is similar to that of the 45th Div. above. However, in this "start-stop, march, fight, and then march again" situation, we have to *deal with both* regular, all leather, buckle up, GI Combat Boots and the "LL Bean type," rubber bottom boot packs. In this contest the boot packs lose out.

They are fine with dry socks sitting in a foxhole, doing nothing, but they are useless for marching or fighting. After any time at all on the road with these rubber marvels one's feet sweat, and the moisture cannot get out through the rubber. Then in a foxhole the sweat freezes and hello trench foot, etc. For 1-2 days this soldier marched and fought in the combat boots, with the boot packs hanging off of his web belt in the rear!!

Then I switched to the boot packs on peaceful nights while the combat boots dried out. Totally impractical, the boot packs were discarded in short order.

The Frozen, Solid White Winter - Continuing the 45th Div. story above

"In the winter, special snow-boots were issued to some troops, but unfortunately not to all those 45th Div. guys fighting in Alsace." By 1944-year-end (510) order of the VI Corps, this soldier of the 1st Battalion, 315th is temporarily attached to the 45th Div. for nine hours on 15 January '45. This was indeed the black morning for me!!

I would be forever grateful to any WW2 buff who can tell me, regarding the 45th Div.: What boots and clothing were they wearing under the fierce artillery barrage? With what picks, shovels, and gear did they dig their foxholes? What were the dimensions and shape of their foxholes? How did they keep their feet from freezing 1205-0600 hours? And finally, were they wearing white capes? Why and why not?

This correspondent waits with bated breath for this "rest of the story" in the northern Vosges of Alsace!

Chapter Ten - Part G
315th Siegfried patrolling North of the Lauter River
Dateline: **Week of Sat.16-23. December 1944 - for the Big Blue '79**
You learn in the "On the Defensive" introduction above that the 313th and 314th Regiments attack the Siegfried Line while the Reserve 315th conducts supporting recon and combat recon patrols.

Our Regimental History reports:

Saturday 16 Dec. In the dark of pre-dawn, the 1st Battalion crosses the Lauter on the engineers foot bridge, meets no opposition, captures two Kraut soldiers sound asleep, and finds that the two large "German Officer" HQ buildings in Scheibenhardt are marked with red crosses in violation of the Geneva Convention.

The 2nd Battalion also crosses pre-dawn, occupies northern Scheibenhardt, and with the assistance of AT Company, constructs the first vehicle bridge for 315th use. The 3rd Battalion also crosses meeting mostly no opposition, while the I & R Platoon (Roger Campbell) gets more than halfway through the forest north of Scheibenhardt encountering no Germans at all, with all bridges intact and no roadblocks. The entire civilian population has been evacuated. 11 prisoners are taken.

Sunday 17 December: The attacking 313th & 314th Regiments encounter the hard Siegfried Defenses which are as advertised. South of the Lauter in area about 625 GI Dog Faces are able to take baths in the Regimental Shower unit located in Neuwiller. USA Paramount News visits Scheibenhardt for a re-enactment of the famous Dewey White crossing. GI's from "B, F & I" Companies go in front of their cameras.

Monday 18 December: 315th remains in reserve while 313th and 314th attack the Siegfried in force, meeting formidable resistance as advertised. Our 315th 1st Battalion, Charlie Company (Jessie Vincent) sends out patrols to the Siegfried encountering rifle and MG fire.

Tuesday 19 December: To assist the advance of the 313th and 314th Regiments our 1st Battalion is given the mission of creating a diversionary attack. It pushes past some tank obstacles but is stopped by direct fire from two pillboxes. The 313th is able to take three pill boxes, only to have these gains wiped out by determined enemy counterattacks, supported by armor. At 1215 and 1600. Prevailing intelligence is the Siegfried Line Pill boxes are manned primarily by Volkssturm, interlaced with regular Wehrmacht soldiers in a rock-solid combination.

Wed. 20 December: 1st Battalion Abel and Baker Companies which had been in contact with the enemy yesterday are withdrawn to Scheibenhardt. This leaves Charlie Company to furnish security for three combat patrols still operating.

Thursday 21 December: During the early morning hours enemy patrols were particularly aggressive, moving their outposts closer to our lines. The 2nd Battalion sends out a patrol which encounters strong hold. Our first scout is captured by a German speaking fluent English, who was killed by our alert second scout, rescuing the first scout. A huge fire fight ensues from what is estimated to be a full, platoon sized enemy force.

Friday 22 December: This is the last day for the Regimental CP in Niederlauterbach, and of the Battalion CP's in Scheibenhardt. The Division order comes down for the 315th to take up an entirely new sector just south of Wissembourg in the vicinity of Riedseltz.

Chapter Ten - Part H
Wissembourg and Vicinity Close out 1944 The enemy Siegfried to the north. Schweigen, Schweighofen, & Kapsweyer to the south Reg. CP Steinseltz, Riedseltz, Geitershoff, down to the Maginot
Dateline: Last Week of Sat.23-30 Dec.1944

For the Big Blue 79 the close out weeks of 1944 are astonishing in the complexity of the interrelationships, day-by-day, of the overall timeline. It is also a crucial week which sets the stage for the even more complex and horrendous, first 3 weeks of 1945. This is the absolute heart of the combat half of Sunshine Soldier. Consider it well as if 'You are there, each day.'

Dateline: Sat 23 Dec 1944 from the Regimental History

Redeployment Orders come down from Division, and the 315th moves by truck about nine miles westward, from Niederlauterbach to Steinseltz-Riedseltz vicinity as described in the header above, prior to darkness on Christmas Eve.

The Regiment is to have set up an amazing, dug in, log/timber/dirt, major defense line! This line stretches out 6-8 miles, west-to-east just south of the east Foret de Wissembourg which is in turn, just south of the Lauter River

All foxholes and positions are to have overhead cover, fully camouflaged. Topics we will cover below include super foxhole deluxe, and Christmas time manning the deep Maginot Bunkers just south of Riedseltz, from Brammelbach, SE to Hunspach.

Hang on tight. It is quite an adventure, now in the solid white, solid frozen landscape of late December. The 1st Battalion CP is set up in Riedseltz, the 2nd in Schweighofen and the 3rd Schweigen, both patrolling outposts in Germany near the Siegfried. In this new alignment, our 315th is flanked on the left by 179th of the 45th Div. and, on the right by the 313th Inf.

Chapter Ten - Part I
Super foxholes deluxe for our GI, Mini-Maginot Contractor:
The Big Blue 79 Construction Battalion, (CB's)
Dateline: Sun. 24 Dec.1944 - We never built one like this at Fort Benning!

Christmas Eve 1944 breaks sunny but cold over the solid white, solid frozen strip of landscape high ground, about 16 square miles (2x8), just south of Route D244 sloping down to the Lauter River Valley to the north. The Regimental staff takes a sober look at this white scene and ponders the Division order to dig in the entire Regiment plus 1-2 Tank Destroyer Battalions.

This is on a frozen strip of farmland. Conservatively, we are talking about… one thousand foxhole positions along with a bevy of huge Tank and Command Control Bunker positions. The "mission impossible" is to dig, cover and camouflage all of these in one day, before dark, and excavate it through ground that is frozen so hard that even a heavy hand pick can hardly touch it.

Much less with the tiny GI tin trenching shovels. Not willing to be branded as 'no-can-do' guys, the Regimental CP shouts can do! Then it pulls out all the stops in Combat Team resources. For all GI's and this soldier correspondent … they come up with the thousand sets of heavy hand picks and shovels, and the heavy 4x6 timbers and railroad ties to support the earthen roofs. For the huge positions they bring all of this... pneumatic jack hammers and air compressors to break through the frozen crust!

Got all of that? Now, let's quit complaining and get on with the job: Freedom for the USA! For a realistic visualization of our mini-maginot let's look in on one of the 1000 foxholes mentioned above, in the 1st Battalion, Baker Co. Sector, 2nd Platoon, 2nd Sgd.

Chapter Ten - Part J
BAR Team Position "Super Foxhole Deluxe"

It is built by the three-man team in our squad, including this soldier correspondent. Except for the separate living and fighting holes, it is fairly typical of most BAR positions. All other positions were one- or two-man teams with their assigned weapons, M-1, Bazooka, 60mm mortars, light & heavy MG's.

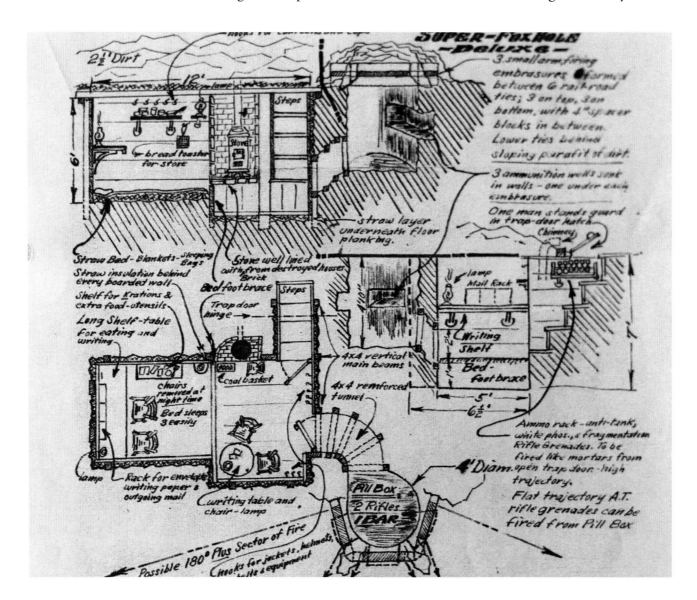

Chapter Ten - Part K
Academic Course foxhole 101 for your education

With the above glimpse of the king of them all, Super Foxhole Deluxe, it is appropriate now to examine the fundamentals essential to a GI's survival at the face of war!

The earth, the deep, rich, black earth, in spite of its stones, roots, rocks, and concrete-like, ice block, frozen crust, is, and always will be, GI Dog Face's best friend!

When he is unfortunate enough to be on top of it, an '88'/artillery barrage can in seconds leave him a remnant of a man, in mind or in body. When he is underneath it, he is safe (except for air bursts… then he needs a solid roof!) In 60 days of combat I have moved and lifted enough of it to foundation a house.

Gone with the Wind are the days in Fort Benning Basic Training when we would 'gold brick' our way out of digging anything resembling a real foxhole. Now we are in the ETO, where men and boys dig with the fury of a leopard, with every incoming shell accelerating this fury like a shot of adrenalin.

Architectural and Civil Engineering triumphs abound in foxhole design. These are the creations of the line Dog Face GI and have been played-up in Bill Mauldin's cartoon series and other State Side publications.

Not long after we penetrated the German border and hit the 'dragon's teeth' of the Siegfried, we all moved back into defensive positions as detailed above. Given all of the heavy lumber, equipment and supplies needed, we decided to take a chance that we might be there for a while, at least. This is clearly no one-night stand. So, we pull out all the stops. We all go out with intentions of building a sub-surface, 'Empire State' building… a regular pill box, a super glorified foxhole. We dub our mini-sector in this 'Mini-Maginot' as the 'Oswald Line'… obviously, the strongest link in the entire 315th Chain. I layout the boundaries of what will soon be our 12x6' living/sleeping room.

Then, with great gusto and profound fanfare, I wind up and take a mighty swing at "White-Faced Mother Earth" with my trusty little tin pie-hoe. The shock and reverberation is heard up and down the entire line a mile away, as the little hoe just bounced 15' into the air spinning like a crazy baton!

Inspection of the damage done reveals a tiny 'piano scratch' in Mother Earth. This frozen crust proves to be a foot thick, and, before the heavy engineering picks arrive we pound away with our toy shovel-pies to no avail. We thanked God that we were not under rifle MG, and artillery attack at the time. This would have been an absolute disaster. Hermann Goering's recon and harassing over flights did not spot us. Astonishing!

Even the heavy picks sink only about an inch into the frozen crust, and this results in an explosion of rock-like shrapnel of frozen earth, flying up in our faces and cutting us up some. This crust stalled the standard 'CAT' bulldozers. These came later come to dig the Tank/TD Bunkers and huge, underground Squad Rooms.

After we back away for about half a day cutting our 6x12' hole, a foot deep in this crust, we stand back in awe and watch the Combat Engineer Battalion plow through it in a matter of seconds with heavy, pneumatic tools, digging holes for TNT charges.

Queried often about what the face of war is like I usually suggest the readers or audience go out in the frozen winter and dig a hole in their front lawn and sleep in it. Amendment No. 1: "Hold the TNT!" The 'Living Room' hole is great, but impossible to fight from. So, we sink in a cylindrical 4-5' diameter, 'Pill Box' Fighting Hole, 4'10' deep in front of the living room. Here we cut, fused and packed our own TNT. Reports are that our 1st and 3rd Army Infantry are issued TNT for digging in on the attack! Good Deal!

This soldier had done a lot of thinking about this super foxhole, so the design is well in mind before we start. After connecting the living room with a short, 3x3' curved tunnel we start cutting out the surface entry steps to get in-and-out of the living hole.

Then we lug the heavy, 15 ft. 4x4' beams and other lumber from a huge lumber pile a mile away. No fun at all! When we cover the Oswald Fort with 3 feet of dirt, we have the beginnings of a darn good hole... Col. Shriver, CO of the 315th, inspects our hole complex and tells us our hole is the best in the whole 1st Battalion. So, we are on cloud nine... but he forgot to acknowledge: it is really the best in the whole dang Regiment.

The living quarters are completely lined with planks from an old, condemned barn we tore down. Main and vertical cross beams are 4x4" timber. Four chairs, a stool, a round table, braces for shelves, three lamps, kitchen utensils, bread toaster, frying pan, stove and pipe, hooks for hanging jackets, belts and equipment... all round out the furnishings.

All other tools and fittings are supplied by a nearby towns of Riedseltz, Geitershoff, Lingolsheim or Seebach. This includes nails, hammer, buck saw, three doors and hinges. Bricks for lining the fireplace are from demolished houses. We have jeeps to help with the heavy stuff. Before the plank roof was covered with dirt, we add an extra thick layer of straw insulation. This was from a stack of bails nearby. The same insulation is used behind the vertical walls and the rough dirt foundation behind.

This treatment really keeps in the heat. 4 GI's can live in the super foxhole comfortably, 3 sleeping and one standing guard. So, for our BAR team!

The curved tunnel, self-supporting, yet still reinforced with 4x4 timbers, curves upward a foot to reach the fighting floor of the Pill Box. Just one hole out of a thousand and a daunting task for our two-man BAR team, yet the sense of accomplishment and sense of humor alone turn the work into pleasure!

Overall, the huge, Regimental 'CB' Construction Battalion work effort is driven by the certainty, yet unknown timing, of the German Operation Nord wind attack sure to come. Imagine if any group of the 21st Century was taken out into the middle of a cold, frozen white, wheat field and told: "This, gentlemen, is where you are going to live and fight for survival".

Chapter Ten - Part L
A White Christmas Story - 1944 - ETO manning the French Maginot line bunkers frozen solid under a 6-12 inch blanket of white powder
Dateline: **Mon.25 Dec.1944 - Towns of Brammelbach, Lingolsheim, & Hunspach**

You had better believe they would treat Christmas in the same way! Turns out, this is indeed our home for the last week of the year, Christmas to New Years, while we patrol and do other jobs. Finally, one thing is sure in the Army: If a Dog Face GI gets the urge to travel... if he is tired of his present environment... then all he has to do is to carry a 75lb. stove on his back from a town a mile away and install it in his foxhole! Within an hour after the first puff of smoke comes out of the stack, guaranteed... the Division order will come down to move out. They'll do it every time!

It is a dark 1800 hours when the low tone drone of a long line of 2 ½ Ton trucks hits our ears not far from our plush accommodations at our Super Foxhole Deluxe.

We are assembled at the 1st Platoon, Baker Company CP Bunker when we get Sgt. Cone's quiet command to load up. As a backup to our 315th Log-Earth-Bunker Line, the 3 Battalions are taking turns manning the Genuine French Maginot Bunkers only 4-5 miles south. We de-truck in Lingolsheim after a short ride in the coldest winter in ETO memory.

'Tis the Night of Christmas, and the time, eleven o'clock late, and not a single shell is landing... not even an eighty-eight! 'Tis Five below zero, and a tad more cozy than minus ten, we are due down in the Maginot, our long line of men.

Silently we follow a well-traveled trail stomped into the snow, as we approach this network of massive now inoperative and obsolete concrete pillboxes and bunkers of the WWl... Our buddies from the 2nd Battalion are ending their 4-hour shift.

To replace them we are led past a line of foxholes chiseled out of the six-inch snow! This on solid frozen earth on a ridge line. Shortly we come to the hole manned by the guy I am to replace. It appears that the ground is not the only thing that is frozen... This poor GI can hardly move but is highly motivated to vacate the dang hole.

I climb into this frosty excuse for a hole with a dim and doubtful, crystalline view to the north, wondering how I am going to pass the next four hours, keep from freezing, and still function. Marching in place, trying to keep warm I peer over the foxhole rim and scan the defensive field of fire out to the north and north east. I had seen worse.

It is a weird, misty white darkness in the lightly falling snow. In this frozen wasteland I am alone with nothing but my thoughts and my other solitary buddies in their holes perhaps 80 feet away, each side. On this Christmas night 1944 the GI's of Baker Company have much to be thankful for. Somehow, someway, incomprehensibly, we are all still alive.

Best of all, there is no incoming artillery. With that usual barrage of concussive, completely debilitating shocks, blasting the woods to shreds all around us and separating our very bodies from our souls.

I contemplate and rehash my first 45 days on the line after leaving Bayonne and Luneville, France, 85 miles to the southwest. I wonder what in the heck is really going on and what the future has in store for all of us. Like all of my GI buddies I know absolutely nothing about the larger war going around us. I am the embodiment of Schultz in the Hogan's Heroes TV 'Back to the future' in reverse, we could be under siege in Bastogne or murdered in Malmedy at this very moment. Now alert! My thought train is interrupted as passwords fill the air in hushed tones, and shadowy images of GI's move about the snowy night and approach my hole. Incredibly my four hours is up, and I am only half frozen. Our squad is being replaced by the next guard shift. So we can bet on four hours of sleep! The time is just after midnight, Tues. 26 Dec. 1944. Time marches on!

Chapter Ten - Part M
The trek down deep to sleep in La Grande Hotel Maginot!

With our guard relief now fully in charge of the bleak line of foxholes this soldier correspondent trudges single file with my squad through a night so cold it can freeze our lungs with each breath. We approach the massive and foreboding steel door of our assigned concrete bunker. We slip into the dark, dank, candle lit interior with some trepidation.

Then we go down, down and keep on going down an ancient steel stairway which finally quits, down in the bowels of the earth. There we enter a maze of concrete rooms, about 15x15ft. Here we are glad to share those hard, damp, cold but above freezing walls and floors with the piles of straw and the local rats.

Under our bed rolls we quickly succumb to a deep sleep! Thence to repeat this 4 hour cycle the balance of Christmas Day. So much for Christmas 1944 on the front lines... Very little talk... and a good deal of praying. No singing… no mail call… no festivities... no nothing. But we are all proud to do it. It is just part of the price of freedom we all enjoy in the 21st Century.

On Wed. 27 Dec. we arrive back in our plush, super foxhole deluxe. We are not entirely thrilled by the accommodations at La Grande Hotel Maginot. In fact, we are glad to let all of the other battalions of the Big Blue 79 take their turn in the Maginot. We had done our share of slumming it and enjoy the five remaining, close out days.

We spend our time in our Hotel Super-Fox, writing and reading war letters on our little round table by lamp light. Oh! Also, we do give Colonel Shriver a reasonable amount of time patrolling the Siegfried Line, just to keep the Germans awake. Operation Nordwind axe will fall next year. It promises to be a doozy.

CHAPTER ELEVEN

Chapter Eleven - Part A

PREFACE REMARKS: The action timeline for this chapter covers the period 1 through 15 January 1945. The primary source documents are war letters written 63 years ago. WW2 is raging everywhere. It is 7 months after D-Day Normandy.

Northern Vosges campaign - Mattstall to Reipertswiller"Rittershoffen" baby Jean-Marie Ober, born Jan. 4, 1945

A heartwarming interlude at the face of war punctuates the horror and sacrifice in the greatest battle of the veteran 315th Infantry in WW2.

The Setting: The bloody combat during Operation Nordwind... The Nazi Counterattack I call... The Battle of the Bulge-South, from the Lauter River, 20 miles south to the Moder River, 25 miles southeast to the villages of Hatten and Rittershoffen, just 10 miles northeast of Haguenau. NE Alsace-Lorraine, France, Jan. 1945.

The Weather: The coldest, most miserable winter in European memory

The Story: Researched and compiled by Les Brantingham, Glynn Welsh and a team of intrepid, veteran explorers of the 315th Infantry Regiment, 79th Division, April 1992, and Ray Kieffer, French Generalkonsulat.

This overview is a mix of my eye-witness memory, as supported by 3rd party firsthand accounts & personal archives from the 315th.

Dateline: Mon.-Wed., 1- 3 Jan.1945 - Riedseltz & Steinseltz, France.

It is an early born, frozen-fingered dawn that breaks on the morning of New Year's Day 1945. We are near the border city of Wissembourg in northeast Alsace, France, on the Lauter River. A pretty and young (23 years old) Alsatian girl, Odile Ober, and her "barber" husband arise. They awaken to another day of pure hell amidst the fighting. This is just prior to the Nazi Operation Nordwind.

At her home, she is a "mother-to-be" just eleven days away from full term. Only 2 miles to the south the Regimental HQ (CP) of the 315th is set up in Steinseltz having arrived there on Dec.23. 1.5 miles to the north the 3rd Battalion, "I" Co. (Glynn Welsh and Wiley Taylor) are in defensive positions in the village of Schweigen, on the Siegfried Line, across the Lauter River in Nazi Germany. With some apprehension they peer northward into enemy territory. This is where Operation Nordwind is brewing!

It is across an Allied Western Front, but for us, on the corner of the French "Teapot," the front runs east-west, not north-south, as is the case for most other units.

This front is in the shape of an enormous zigzag. Up north and east, starting on Dec. 16, the Battle of the Bulge-North is now raging. In the past The Wehrmacht has pushed an 80-mile bulge eastward into Allied lines, well into Bastogne in Belgium.

Down south, the US Seventh Army (including the 79th and 45th Divisions) has pushed and equally daunting bulge eastward into German Lines, clear to Lauterbourg on the Rhine ... a full 120 miles EAST of Bastogne. Most historians seem to have forgotten this Battle of the Bulge-South. At this point, elements of the 315th have crossed the Lauter River from Wissembourg to Lauterbourg. These units are the first into Germany and have "bulged" the furthest east of all Allied Forces... by a big bunch!!!

Even as he is being pushed back inch by inch up North, Hitler clearly wants to change all of this via Operation Nordwind. He wants to chomp off the whole Allied southern bulge and thus destroy the entire US 7th Army, from Wissembourg to Strasbourg. He is not to succeed. Reason is the mettle of the dog-face GI's of the 79th including the 315th.

Yes, Odile, Charles and "baby to be" Ober are caught smack in the middle of this whole insane mess, in an insane war! They cross paths with this soldier correspondent, unseen on route D264 in Riedseltz. This was just 2 mi. to the east of his Super Foxhole Deluxe! A pure random coincidence at war's face.

Dateline: **Mon.-Wed., 1- 3 Jan. 1945 - Riedseltz, Steinseltz, Soultz sous Forets, 1st Battalion.**
In Riedseltz the 1st Battalion Unit Journal logs that the night skies had been punctuated with red, white and yellow flares. At 0605 hrs. a returning Charlie Co. patrol reports 15 enemy tanks near the railroad station, with light and heavy vehicular traffic. At 0652 hrs. Baker Co. reports a tank firing from the wood facing their position, azimuth 60 deg. from 2nd Platoon.

At 0833 hours Charlie Co. Traffic Control point reports 63 vehicles but no civilians all night long. Situation is quiet during day of Jan. 1. At 1800 hrs the 315th 1st Battalion receives orders from Corps. HQ to move west to Zinswilller to be attached to the 45th Div. At 1700 hrs. Jan. 2nd the 315th Reg. HQ & CP is moved from Steinseltz back to Soultz. 7 mi. to the SSW.

Awakening in Wissembourg on the frosty morning of Jan. 3 Odile and Charles Ober realize that the Americans had pulled out of their positions near and north of the Lauter, blowing all of the bridges over the Lauter from Wissembourg to Lauterbourg.

In the grip of a pervasive, stark, nerve-rattling fear the couple decides to head south on foot toward Riedseltz where she had been checked out. Many civilians fleeing the fighting had to be turned back out of military necessity. But, after lengthy discussions, the Ober's were allowed to continue south. Ultimately, this proves to be a day long journey trudging on frozen feet through the worst ice and snow imaginable! At 1700 hours they arrive beat-up, frozen, and exhausted in Schoenenbourgj 7 mi. to the south, and in the vicinity of Hatten & Rittershoffen. Mind you... the gal is right at full term!

They are now only a mile away from the new Reg. CP in Soultz, just south of the Siegfried. They are just 2 miles away from the new defensive positions of "I" Co. in Birlenbach, to which the 3rd Battalion had been withdrawn. At the face of war, everything happens in the miserable, dark, black, frozen, wee hours.

Dateline: Wed., 3 Jan. 1945 Riedseltz & Schoenenbourg, on the Ober's trek south
Strangers in Schoenenbourg watch with some apprehension as Odile & Charles trudge by. These observers have no clue as to where the couple is going, but she is obviously pregnant! They kindly take in the Obers, feed them, and give them a briefly cozy place to rest.

Barely settled down in the warmth at 2030 hrs. the labor pains begin... hastened by the arduous trip south. Charles quickly decides their best bet is the 2nd Battalion Aid Station, set up in a house on rue des Vergers, flying the Red Cross flag. As Odile and Charles hasten their way to the Aid Station along rue Bische they are passed by a jeep ambulance. It carries two stretchers with wounded. They follow the jeep to the beautiful Red Cross flag, arriving at 2300 hours. It is their "Longest Day" and their welcome flag is waving just outside the Aid Station sanctuary of the 1st Battalion, 315th.

Dateline: Thur. 4 Jan. 1945 - Schoenenbourg, not Rittershoffen ... is the place!
A tad past midnight. it is 0010 hrs ... what else did you expect? On site the doctor, Capt. Charles Dowell of Carrollton, Ohio (20 miles SE of Canton) makes the initial examination. Pains of 'good quality' at 1 to 3 min. intervals, completely dilated... fetal tones completely normal! Absolutely remarkable under the miserable, insane circumstances... the 'little finger' of God is surely with the Ober's. Clearly, no time for evacuation by ambulance. The birth had to take place on-site!

He quickly sets up a makeshift delivery room, assembles a small team, chases out all non-professional kibitzers. This war scene is beyond the imagination. Bombastic incoming & outgoing artillery shells shake and rattle the building! At 0045 hrs., by the light of two kerosene lamps and a flashlight the epic "Rittershoffen" baby is born in Schoenenbourg but reported to the entire US Army erroneously by the "Stars and Stripes" news as having been born in Rittershoffen. In the fog of war, this is an understandable, 4-mile error!

The medical team of this "Mini-MASH" mighty 315th is a pure melting pot from all over the USA Anesthetist, 2nd Lt. Frank Sadowski of Twin Lakes, Wisconsin; orderlies: T-3 Harold Silverman of Gary, Indiana, T-4 Julius Beard of Columbia, Miss., and T-4 Albert Connors of Mechanicsville, Iowa. The irreverent kibitzers are invited back shortly thereafter for a look-see.

"My God" says one, "It's a skinned rabbit!"

"Like hell" answers Capt. Dowell, "It's a boy… six and a half pounds of him." Just then the boy cuts loose with one of his first, full-throated, fortissimo yells.

"Listen to that" says another GI, "He bellers (bellows) like a first sergeant!

So, they all want to christen him "Topkick!"

But new mother, Odile Ober isn't buying this for a minute. She names him Jean-Marie Ober! New father, Charles Ober, not knowing how to thank the Americans, finally offers free haircuts to the entire Medical Team.

A GI interpreter stays with Odile all night long and early on Jan. 4th she is evacuated 19 miles south to Brumath, and hence another 10 miles south to the Midwives College in Strasbourg. Finally, she stays with her uncle in Tivoli, Italy, until April 1945, just a month before VE Day.

Fast forward 51 years to June 1996. Ten members of the West family, including 2 babies (24 and 27 months) are met by Jean-Marie and his wife at the Paris, Orly Airport. At their Orly home we have a nice, two family visit. He drives us all over Paris. The next week, with the help of Lise Pommois we visit mother Odile at her home near Niederbronn.

Chapter Eleven - Part B
The Northern Vosges Campaign… Mattstall to Lichtenberg and Reipertswiller
Dateline: Timeframe -Mon. 1 Jan., through Mon.15 Jan. 1945
Background - Regimental History

The year opens with a bang and big trouble. We long expected the Nazi Operation Nordwind assault on the entire northern Vosges front from Lauterbourg to Bitche. It is believed that the Nazis have thrown no less than seven Infantry Divisions & one Motorized Division into the area. This includes the 6th SS Mountain Division. Wolf T. Zoepf from this Division wrote a book "Seven Days in January."

It describes a deep penetration, combat patrol he went on in these seven days. For this correspondent, fate does indeed arrange a confrontation with a sniper from this delightful outfit on a frozen 15 Jan.

The Germans also have two Panzer Divisions and a Motorized Division in reserve. The threat gets far worse. As mentioned above, Operation Nordwind (the Battle of the Bulge-South) also includes a southern pincer to cross the Rhine, & bite off the entire US 7th Army: Strasbourg, from Gambsheim to Druesenheim. So, guys… we now have a two-front war on our hands!

With Hitler's massive forces now deployed against the US 7th Army, on 2 fronts, all the way from Gambsheim to Bitche an imminent attack of major proportions can readily be seen. This conflict divides into three, very nasty zones to be treated separately:

The Gambsheim Pincer across the Rhine

The Epic Battle of Hatten and Rittershoffen, Lauter River: Wissembourg to Lauterbourg

The Northern Vosges Mountain Campaign, westward from Wissembourg to Bitche

By the grace of God, this soldier correspondent escaped the first two, scot-free. But He really nailed me for the third. The "What if? connotations are abundant! To meet this threat an amazing array of US Divisions, Regiments, and support units are deployed from east-west. The saga of these units is superbly covered by Lise Pommois in her book "Winter Storm," starting with "A Decisive Day."

They are centered in the Reipertswiller Lichtenberg area. They include the 361st VGD and a Combat Group of the 6th SS Mountain Division, called Combat Group Schreiber. Our US Combat Group is called the 315th Infantry Regiment under Col. Schriver. In the world melting pot, it sounds like German vs. German. This seems reasonable and follows a trend, since the SHAEF HQ is headed by a guy named "Eisenhower!".

Our 315th CO, Col. Schriver's S2 (Intell. officer), Lise Pommois' assessment, the 79th Div. G2, and our Corps G2 … all agree! All along the 36 miles, west to east front, stretching out from Bitche to Lauterbourg, a major attack is anticipated. The 79th ID (Infantry Division) and 45th ID would no doubt be called on at some time, very soon. We just didn't know in which sector the major brunt of the attack would come. The 11-mile eastern sector of Rittershoffen? Or the 25 mi., western sector of the Northern Vosges? The answer is of course both, concurrently and big-time!

Later in the book, the western Northern Vosges Sector, and the eastern Rittershoffen Sector will be covered.

Chapter Eleven - Part C
First Battalion unit journal history
Dateline: **Timeframe -Mon. 1 Jan., through Mon.15 Jan. 1945**

All battalions of both USIDs would be called on to share the load, and starting 1 Jan. They order the 315 first Battalion (my "B" Co.) to be sent westward to help out the 45th Div. in the Northern Vosges Sector, while the 2nd and 3rd Battalions will stay behind to fight in the Rittershoffen Sector.

Jan. 2, Crossing paths with the Ober's (in the "Baby of Rittershoffen" story) the day after they started their trek south, this soldier correspondent heads west for Mattstall patrols with the 1st Battalion.

On Jan. 3 at 0015 hours we move out by truck & close in (arrive) at Zinswiller at 0245. Jan.3. We of Baker Co. remain there during the night to establish roadblocks with Charlie Co. About fifteen artillery shells fired from tanks land on Zinswiller and vicinity during the night. At 1400 hours we entruck to Mattstall, arrive at 1530, & relieve the 2nd Battalion, 180th Reg., 45th Div. by 1730. By 2240 "D" Co. reports friendly artillery falling on their positions, bummer!

Jan. 4, We start vital recon & combat patrols. All along the northern front we have to find out what the Nazis are up to.

Chapter Eleven - Part D
The "Mad Hatters" patrols to Dusseldorf

On Jan. 6 we launch our memorable series of excursions NW of Lembach. They take us up the steep, heavily forested trail into the mountains NW to the town of Disteldorf. This needs a "Battle Scale map" planned for future editions of Sunshine Soldier. Even more memorable is our 1996 West family "mad hatters" fast ride up the very primitive & bumpy dirt road in a "jeep-like" vehicle. Lise Pommois is with us, hanging on for dear life, it was a fitting and proper retrace of the 1945-foot patrols by this soldier correspondent. We finally arrive at the 3-5 houses in Dusseldorf as I marvel that they are still there and happy at not being shot at! Lise gives us a proper tour.

Jan. 4, at 0800 hrs. our Baker Co. contacted, reported and dispersed a German patrol. At 2020 the 645th TD (Tank Destroyer) Bo joined us with much appreciated help.

Jan. 5, at 0735 "A" Co. reports and disperses a 15-man German combat patrol trying to enter town of Lembach.

Jan. 6 three special, eight-man patrols, ''Poison" (a code name) 1, 2, & 3 are dispatched. They report enemy vehicular traffic in 1st Battalion sector. Later at 1100 hrs our Charlie Co. combat patrol reports a 3-man German Patrol near Dusseldorf Saints above... that is just a tad away, off in the woods. But the "clowns" evade our patrol and escape.

At 1300 my Baker Co. patrol actually engages a 9-man enemy patrol in Dusseldorf. A fire fight ensues & we prudently withdraw. But it established that this town is a "metropolis" of 3-4 houses is clearly in contention in Nordwind. At 1730 Seven Italians were taken by "A" Co. They claim they are forced to labor for the Germans. At 2300 "A" Co. also reports same harassing Nazi 88mm artillery fire as earlier.

Jan. 7, at 0305 hrs. my Baker Co., 1st Platoon reports the sound of an enemy plane flying over the 1st Bo. Sector. It seems the Luftwaffe is far from dead. In a showdown at Disteldorf, a Baker Co. Combat Patrol #1 is planned, of two squads (24 men). Their mission is to eliminate the enemy and/ or take prisoners at Distledorf.

Jan. 8 All Reports are negative until midnight.

Jan. 9 0135 hrs. Baker Co. reports the sound of armor ... two German tanks, pulling into Disteldorf, stopped with their motors running. By 0305 hrs. the tanks have shut down! By 0705 they start up their motors again. Then patrols indicate all enemy armor is gone.

Jan. 9 and 10 Enemy activity elsewhere near Lembach during the two nights. Then on Jan. 10 at 0125 hrs. "Poison" 3 (code name) starts reporting to 1st Battalion HQ every hour. Patrol# 3 spots a seven-man German patrol working down the road to Lembach, also observed by the 36th Engineers. At 0800 hrs. all three companies send out patrols. They meet dug in Nazis & are involved in some fire fights.

Jan.11 is the Last day of Patrols. At the end of the first 10 days in January... there are no battle casualties in the 1st Battalion. Amazing!

Chapter Eleven - Part E
1st Battalion heads to Zinswiller & Reipertswiller

Jan. 12 at 2135 hrs. out 1st Battalion 315th Inf. Reg., 79th Div. is notified that it is to relieve the 2nd Battalion 276th Inf. Reg., 45th Div.

Jan. 14 at 1800 hrs. we depart via truck to Reipertswiller and the Castle of Lichtenberg, closing in on the Mountain Jan. 15 at 0030 hrs. to put the relief in place.

Chapter Eleven - Part F
A percussion symphony – "the night before"

The rest of the night the Battalion is pounded by a horrific nightmare of Nazi artillery & mortar fire, including 220mm (8.7") rockets! It is a ghastly scene silhouetted in lightning-like, explosive flashes of the incoming, air-bursting artillery shells! These shatter and shake the earth itself! On frozen, rocky slopes, flying, zinging, jagged hunks of steel rip the trees to shreds. In a myriad of zinging trajectories the shrapnel shards fly.

They end their murderous journeys with solid, sickening "thunks" into tree trunks. With each "thunk" we all heave a sigh of relief that, for this one, it is not buried in human flesh! This incoming mayhem pounds our very souls with the persistent message, that… If we do not dig in quick, we will all be shredded as well, and dead before we even get to sleep! Otherwise… things are quite peaceful. But then again… we can't sleep anyway. A tad difficult in the pervasive nightmare and ominous, swishing aerodynamics of high velocity, incoming artillery. Each explosion is followed by a blinding night flash, and bone jarring shock. They are coming in with absolutely unnerving frequency.

We can't really dig in either. The lifeline for WW2 GI's is a small, folded sheet metal, trenching tool that unfolds to a 30" shovel, or folded again at 90 degrees, it becomes a 24" chopping pie/hoe. One thousand of these shovel picks are rebounding off of frozen earth and stones… all over the mountain!

A deadly and hopeless fight, this is a percussion symphony! It is played by a thousand of Mauldin's "Willy and Joes," directed by the devil himself, at the gates of Hell. The "musical instruments" are the nearly useless, tin shovel picks. Needed, but not at hand, are pneumatic jackhammers. The tin shovel picks fly into the air at all crazy angles with zero progress, as we try to penetrate the frigid petrified crust.

Shovels bounce, bend, brake, smash and clash in the unforgettable sounds of young, teenage kids fighting for survival. In my area the clatter of a whole platoon of some thirty-six GI's, simultaneously whacking at that damnable mountain defy mortal description. Maybe by 0130 hours on the 15th I get through the crust and scrape out a vertical hole (not horizontal) barely big enough to get my feet into, and barely deep enough, in a twisted crouch, to get my steel helmet just below the parapet rim. There is no room for my Browning Automatic Rifle (BAR). It is either me or the BAR to go in the hole, but not both. The BAR loses and goes horizontal… up on the rim of the foxhole.

What happens next, in the wee small hours that morning does not easily come to my brain. For all thirty-six of us, total exhaustion has set in. The constant incoming shells relent. I finally doze off… if you can believe this reality at the face of war. First light emerges finally to end this nightmare. I find my head is not blown off by shrapnel, but the stock of my BAR is! All that remains is a jagged piece of black plastic at the aft end of the weapon. It will still shoot... but not from the shoulder… only from the hip.

Back now to the shot that proves to be my second birthday! This shot also really does indeed change my life forever. Picking up on the Jan 15 "Morning of Murderous Mayhem," it is now about 0800 hrs. Emerging from our hell holes, those of us still alive form up and move up the ridge to reinforce the 3rd Platoon.

The frozen morning air is still bursting alive with the very heavy artillery, mortar and small arms fire from the repeated counterattacks by the 6 SS Mountain Div. There is also the intermittent crack of enemy sniper fire.

Chapter Eleven - Part G
The shot that changes my life

Sgt. Cone asks me and my busted BAR to fill in between two, light 30 caliber machine gun positions. I crawl out there ten yards into the frozen mist and trees full of Nazi Snipers.

At 0900 hrs. I poke my head up a tad too far trying to survey the field of fire. At the same time, I must have moved or twitched in the last instant ... or God's little finger moves to nudge the muzzle of the sniper rifle a tiny scant millimeter or two... I don't know which. Perhaps both.

In any event it is in this last instant before the shot rings out in the frozen white, snow-blind perspective. It is a field spotted with not so frozen snipers in the 6th SS Mt. Div., all in white camouflage suits. They are deliberately aiming at the neck carotids or spines of all GI's in our unit! Later I am to find out they killed our Platoon Guide outright. In retrospect, my sense is that the sniper was a lousy shot and missed the above "sure kill" targets. I must have made an "unanticipated" move just before he squeezes off the round.

Chapter Eleven - Part H
The rest of the story

If you want to know what a deer feels like when hit by a high-powered hunting rifle ... listen up and I will tell you, firsthand. It is an overpowering crack; an explosive sound louder than one would ever believe. An instant pervasive numbness permeates my entire upper left shoulder, torso and neck. The large inertia forces involved knock me into a twisting motion, flipped over on my stomach again. I am now crawling for my life back to a safer position with the guys of my squad.

I sure as heck know I am hit ... but I don't know where.

In a few seconds, the horrified looks on my buddies faces tell me all I didn't need to know! I approach them over those ten yards with blood gushing out of my left external jugular. Almost from the instant my body recoils from the impact if that round... I dig in my elbows for the crawl back, auto-reflexes take over.

Chapter Eleven - Part I
"Dear God, not now..."

They are born of my 19 years of Christian training in home, in Sunday school and church, by Christian parents determined to bring me up accordingly. Before my cracked larynx swells up, I mouth four words "Dear God, not now!" They may have been silent, a whisper or an audible shout... I know not which: These four words would change my life forever.

This totally reflexive prayer is rather presumptuous!!! We must all concede, for a scruffy young teenager exactly six months away from his 20th year on this planet. Why shouldn't I die right then and there? Along with Bob Shane, and all the rest of my 400,000 dead WW2 buddies, shot, shredded & blown all to hell? This, along with the thousands of others fighting tyranny all over the world I address our Lord in 'shorthand.' At the face of war there is no time for the Longhand: "Dear Jesus Christ, Son of God and my Savior... not now." I trust the majority of Christians will concede these longhand words will never come out of any Christian mouth in the heat of battle! There isn't time. Only a few milliseconds are available to evoke reactive words from the soul!

It is my covenant with Him, & the strength of my sacred mission for the rest of my life: To speak for my 400,000 dead GI buddies, who cannot speak for themselves!

Chapter Eleven - Part J
Quick medic response and "MASH" evacuation
Dateline: **Mon.15 Jan.1945, Reipertswiller Mt. North of The Castle of Lichtenberg**

At 0900 hrs. on this fateful morning in January, so it is that I crawl out of the danger area within the sniper's sights so "Medico," (our comic Platoon Medic), could help me without being a second casualty himself. From then on it is a case of some darn fast, efficient work on the part of some real solid GI buddies.

These and extra medics are available only because we are in a temporary lull, in the middle of a bitter fire fight with a determined Nazi 6th SS Mountain Div. By my side with "Medico" and two other medics is our Baker Company CO. (Commanding Officer) He is a young 2nd Lieutenant from the Fort Benning Infantry OCS School who had only recently taken over the Company.

Medico used to wear a genuine, tall, black top hat on road marches to the absolute delight of all the roadside French kids.

While "Medico" is applying a direct pressure bandage around my neck (no tourniquets here!) the Lieutenant reassures me that call had been wired back to the Battalion Aid Station three minutes ago. The litter bearers are on their way up the hill. It seems God had a little help here!

Five guys volunteer to sled me all the way down the frozen mountain to meet the litter squad halfway up. They do this with a GI Blanket and two poles whacked out of the woods ... all this time with "Medico" using direct pressure on to my wound to slow the blood loss. The litter squad finds an Alsatian teenager's snow sled in the woods and loads me on it.

Then they control my slow descent down the mountain, all the way to a 4-litter rack jeep, waiting for me on the road below. It is probably 0920 hrs.15 Jan 1945: (GSW=Gunshot Wound+ 20 min). I start my splendid, "MASH style" evacuation! Really quite sporty in Jan.1945. Right on que, the Battalion Aid Jeep starts down on this steep mountain road. My neck wound is obvious, so these guys don't mess around!

I sense an oncoming 'mad hatters' ride! The jeep has special bracket welded to each side. My stretcher is strapped on a bracket and, zingo, I am off with some hair-raising dispatch down the wild and winding road into Reipertswiller & delivered to the 1st Battalion Aid Station. My time estimate at about 0925 [GSW + 25 min].

There are no 1980 TV, MASH helicopters here- impractical in this terrain but the dispatch is every bit the hustle of the TV show. These guys really move! After a new dressing & some warm dry socks (wow they feel good), I am off in a full-fledged USA Ambulance to the clearing station. From there I am off to the Field Hospital, probably in Engwiller. This is on the main road east to Haguenau on the Moder River. My time estimate at about 0930 [GSW + 30 min]. Here I get emergency surgery and stay for 3 days. Ending about Jan.18

By this time, although the swelling in my neck had continued, my wild, whooping, gasping for air is stabilized a bit. Speech is impossible. I can complain only in a forceful whisper and with hand signals. These guys don't mess around either. The MASH units are ordinarily set up in huge canvas tents, but this unit is in warm dry building!

With clock like precision they wheel me into a preparation room. 'Florence Nightingales' surely straight out of Heaven, cut off my clothes, confiscate all my personal goodies. I complain mightily about this to no avail. They give me shots and zap me into the operating room. The total elapsed time from the crack of the sniper rifle? But I doubt if it is over twenty to thirty minutes.

This saves my life! I have the benefit of an excellent surgeon, a young AMC (Army Medical Corps) Captain, also straight out of Heaven. He quickly makes a huge incision, not quite from ear to ear, but darn near. It is, a long, 4 inch slit across my throat, from my larynx up towards my left ear. This connects the entry and exit point of the sniper round to expose all of the concealed damage.

What he finds is sobering indeed. The round rips through an area where it could have done enormous permanent damage in any number of ways. But, guided by the little finger of God it misses all of these by very small fractions of an inch. It takes out my left external jugular vein and several other vessels nearby which he now ties off.

They will still be tied off 63 years later in 2008. In a life and death, mini-mini close call the Nazi sniper round takes a neat notch in the sheath surrounding the carotid artery. If there had been another thirty-second of an inch (about a millimeter) of movement by me at the last instant; or, if a fly had landed on the barrel of the sniper rifle as the trigger was squeezed... the ramifications would have been catastrophic. Presto... I would have been spurting blood several feet as I crawled back to 'Medico.' I call this close! It understandably changes my life forever on this, my second birthday. It also narrowly misses my trachea, esophagus, & most fortunate of all... it misses my spinal cord.

The round also slices through the cartilage tissue surrounding the larynx, cracking things and doing enough damage that the medical staff really don't know if I would ever be able to talk or sing again.

This single factor will have implications, 63 years hence. I can't talk for a week, and really don't know if I would ever do so. What an awful week of trauma & apprehension. This PTS (post-traumatic stress syndrome) first surfaces 35 years later. Most notably, this happens when I am in the Knox Presbyterian Church of Hyde Park in Cincinnati at the funeral of my father-in-law, Pop Winter. I am to learn I simply cannot sing in any church, or at any memorial services of any kind without breaking down completely, sobbing beyond control.

I am seated just behind my four, sharp, wonderful, nightingale daughters. They are singing together at the top of their lungs in full control. What a quartet! They live and they exist in this world... only by the grace of the little finger of God in WW2. No way can I handle this then. No way can I handle it now in 2008. I tear up as I write this.

To those who doubt the credibility of this PTS that simply won't quit. I suggest they go out and get themselves shot as I was. Then see how they handle it. I don't like to cry in public or in church, so

I avoid formal services. It is painful, mortifying and embarrassing. I don't need this. Today, my surviving buddies WW2 vets are passing away like flies… left and right!

So … In whatever time God gives me, I need to spend it writing my book, speaking for my dead GI buddies! Hence, my church going and my prayers to God are in private.

My hospital evacuation train ride, down through Haguenau, and Strasbourg to the 45th General Hospital in Besancon, France.

CHAPTER TWELVE

PREFACE REMARKS: The primary source documents for this chapter are testimonials of other men from the 315th.

Hatten and Rittershoffen... Operation Nordwind The mighty Battle of the Bulge, South
Eye-witness accounts from others in the 315th
Dateline: **Thurs.18 Jan. 1945, 46th General Hospital, Besancon, France**

This day in January I can listen to the US Armed Forces radio and get my first inkling of what happened to my Baker Co. on Jan.17, two days after I was hit, the notorious Battle of Hatten & Rittershoffen, just north of the Haguenau Forest. But it takes my trip to the St. Louis, MO, NPR National Archives in 2002 to finally develop the rest of the story...

"The day we lost Baker Company." This story includes: "The Valiant Eighty MIA's of Rittershoffen. I finally learn that most of my "B" Co. were either killed, wounded or captured in the town!

Dateline: **Time Frame: Mon. 1 Jan., through Tues. 23 Jan. 1945**

It is a story brought to life in the 79th Div. DVD "What Price Freedom." This was taped in 2002 and 2003 in Milwaukee and Chicago. The key testimony by Don Weiskopff, my assistant BAR man as I was hit, and by Lt. Howard Hull. They are, at this writing, the only two survivors of the 'Valiant Eighty' known to be alive.

It is the dramatic saga of my "Busted BAR," and how Weiskopff bravely picks up the ball and runs with it. Only a short wink after I start my snow sled ride down that solid frozen mountain. So, totally unknown to me, as I am being evacuated south in comfort to friendly hands, Hull & Weiskopff are already headed to POW Stalags in Germany.

A tribute to all 315th men from Col. Schriver

In a fitting tribute to the entire Hatten and Rittershoffen saga and the valiant men who fought there, we bring these closing remarks by our Col. Schriver, CO of the 315th... I quote directly from his Regimental History narrative, dated 21 January 1945.

"At 0500, 21 January 1945, after almost 12 days, the greatest battle of the veteran 315th Infantry in World War II ended. The end, though welcome, was distasteful to those men who, despite continuous and heavy pressure from an enemy superior in numbers, stayed and held Hitler's best to limited penetration, instead of the much-desired breakthrough.

The withdrawal was definitely not a defeat to those, who at times held through sheer guts alone. Instead, it was these same men, now withdrawing, who had administered defeat after defeat on an enemy using the latest equipment. But military necessity required that the withdrawal be made.

Particularly distasteful was the fact that the springboard for the attack was the ground these same men had so recently taken after hard fighting. This ground too had to be given up due to enemy pressure in other sectors in the Northern Vosges."

"Only those veterans of Casino, Stalingrad, Rittershoffen & Hatten can understand the clashing of 2 giants in see-saw street fighting, and the stress & strain on human endurance involved. Much credit for the successful defense was due to the 310th Field Artillery Battalion, whose alertness shown in answering calls for fire. They also are credited for repeated procurement of reinforcing artillery Bos. This helped much in warding off the attacking 'Supermen.' Credit, too, goes to those TD's from the 813th and 827th TD Battalions who stayed with our men on defense. Credit also to those elements of the 14th Armored Div. who fought side by side with us in defense & counterattack." -- Colonel Shriver, CO of the 315th Regiment

Chapter Twelve – Part A
"Alsatian Confrontation" by Joseph Kane, Co. F, 2nd Battalion, 315th Jan. 8-21, 1945.

This confrontation ultimately involves all three battalions of the 315th. What was it like to be in Hatten and Rittershoffen during these 12 horrific days? Joe Kane answers this question with an intensive, realistic, first person anecdote. It penetrates the thoughts, fears, frustrations, anxieties and traumas of those valiant and un-faultable teenagers who fought there. Even though still in draft form it really begins to cast into concrete the true face of war - one of the best and most gripping I have yet seen:

"The recent issues of the fraternal and veterans' magazines have numerous articles about incidents, battles, encounters & military actions pertaining to WW2. Many of these articles have been written by authors, writers, editors and researchers who have, very accurately, tracked down the data and have put it into good readable, true accounts of these actions. However, there have been very few first-person narratives. This due to the reluctance of veterans not wanting publicity and feeling that they are not qualified to enter the writing arena. So, I felt it might be of some interest to try to explain the thoughts, actions, the maneuvers, and the frustrations felt by the infantry soldier in time of battle.

The 2nd Battalion of the 315th Infantry, 19th Div. was committed to the attack on Hatten (about 2000 population, in Alsace, France. Their mission was to rescue the remnants of the 42nd Div. Rainbow plus various Tank Destroyer (TD) units, and to be a bulwark against the ongoing attacks by German army units,

For 12 straight days, from January 8, the enemy made the 315th change from offensive to defensive. We had to contend with nightmarish actions such as Krauts in GI uniforms, German flame throwing tanks shooting fire in basements, fire from windows of houses on streets thought to be secured, and machine gun crews in ambulances.

This, plus, nightly patrols in white sheets to camouflage against the snow. We came from Rittershoffen to Hatten (4 miles) in the dusk of Jan. 8 and encountered no serious opposition other than a few mortar rounds, sporadic machine gun (MG) fire. We settled in a corner of Hatten by an apple orchard not far from the railroad. We immediately went on patrol (a few blocks), set up guards as usual, and used every blackout precaution.

This, so they can be as unnoticed as possible. We were amazed at the condition of the buildings which had practically no damage, and we appreciated the opportunity to have a building for shelter. Some civilians (maybe 100) were still living in Hatten, mostly holed up in basements of houses near the typical church in the center of town.

On the morning of January 9, we advanced to the center of town Our Co. "F" was the lead company in the 2nd Battalion of about 700 men. We settled guards in the barns, out- buildings and houses on a small hill overlooking a small orchard and parallel street 300-400 feet away. We observed many German soldiers going in and out of the houses of the adjoining area,

We had a field day picking them off with our M-1 rifles, with only a small amount of return fire. We figured this was one of their main command posts (CP's). Late in the afternoon we received quite a bit of mortar fire, but word came down that we had the enemy surrounded. That night all hell broke loose! They deliberately allowed us to come in… and then surrounded us… with some of the best infantry. Panzer, and grenadier divisions of the German army. These were the lower segments of the southern bulwark of northern Battle of the Bulge.

As of that night they attacked and infiltrated our positions, and "F" Co. was isolated from the rest of the Battalion Our squad was cut off from the Co. CP, and all outside contact was lost. Our squad held our position for 3 days and nights before a flame throwing tank came in from hell and burned our barn and house. We fell back another block to another house/barn complex, typical of Alsace housing. The nights seemed to last at least weeks long. The artillery fire was intense, and the tanks prowled all night firing at everything moving… and not moving! Gomez and I were on guard when we heard something coming. We prepared to fire and saw a horse and just felt easier.

(Now get this Nazi mind set to fully grasp the true inner nature of Hitler's war machine.)

The German tank deliberately sighted on this horse, fired and hit him with an explosive shell that disintegrated him! We were hit with horsemeat and blood all over the place. We had no rations for two days, so Shorter and I headed back to where there were some K-Rations. The problem was we had to cross a street where the crossfire prevented any access. On the way back Shorter did not run fast enough. He was hit in the leg & we pulled him back. He could not be evacuated & didn't make it out of Hatten (meaning sure dead, HW).

The enemy had the street zeroed in and it separated us from the rest of "F" Co., but my box of K-rations arrived safely in spite of their tank fire. It gave us something to eat for a spell, while we were deciding what our next move should be. We had no outside tank support, no air or artillery support, & we were completely surrounded.

We continue to be pounded by enemy artillery barrages. The buildings we were occupying were being knocked down and systematically burned! This forces us to continually fall back, street by street! Ed. Note: Other than this, things were just hunky-dory!

One-night Bob, who had a bazooka, found some rounds ammo for it! He told me to load it and we would give them a big surprise. We knocked down the walls of an enemy held house across the street. We were just congratulating ourselves when they returned fire with a greater bazooka (Nebelwerfer) fire than we had. Catastrophe! This split Bob's face from ear to chin, seriously wounded two other men from our squad, and again made us move, as the house was reduced to rubble.

About the 8th day we were still holding out and had been reunited with our Company. We were using cellars, and only the first-floor guard duty, and firing offensively to keep the Krauts from completely overrunning us. On this date "someone" was looking after this writer (Joe Kane), as he had been sitting on a crate in the cellar.

He got up, Sgt. Smith immediately sat down, and then shrapnel came in through the window opening, killing him instantly. I was about to go on guard duty, but Frank M. asked me to swap time. Ten minutes later Frank was hit in both legs with more shrapnel. Next, a large enemy shell landed on the first floor. Jim Jones and I thought it was a dud and threw it outside where it exploded a few min. later, making a large crater in the street!

I needed a cup of coffee to quiet my nerves, but my canteen was empty, so a trip outside was in order. The barnyard was being shelled periodically, so after six rounds came in, I made a mad dash to the pump and *brought back a pail of water to the house. A civilian boy about 15 saw me return safely so he ventured out, made just one pull on the pump handle! The civilian boy was hit directly by a shell, blowing him to pieces!*

Finally, the powers that be recognized that our Battalion was in dire peril. An airstrike was ordered but was aborted due to bad weather! Only one plane does drop rations, ammo and medical supplies. These fell into enemy hands. The US tank battalion that was dispatched to help us was quickly knocked out.

Dateline: Sun., 21 Jan. '45- The tiny town of Hatten. Corps says enough of this insanity!

The next night was one long to be remembered. The enemy released a two-hour barrage of artillery which further reduced buildings to more rubble. Kraut tanks prowled through the streets covered with bricks, parts of roofs, houses, dead animals and humans, both civilians and soldiers, American and German.

Our 2nd Battalion was now squeezed into a tiny area (about the size of a baseball park) We had suffered so many casualties killed, wounded and captured, that by this final night the withdrawal order comes down from the 6th Corps. At 2300 a very uncoordinated withdrawal along the railroad tracks began with great misgivings about the probable success. Very fortunately for us the enemy had pulled back that night, to regroup for another push! This would have been disastrous for us. But now, their regrouping allowed us to escape. There were less than 400 of us, out of the original 700, who made it out of Hatten, and there was not one house left standing undamaged, or over 10 ft. high.

To attempt to describe the thoughts, feelings, fears and reactions while engaged in this battle is very difficult. For 12 days and nights GI Joe is under Hitler's Nordwind, insane war. Fear is a constant companion. To reassure yourself by saying "A coward dies a thousand deaths, a hero dies but once" wears itself out after a while.

Our 2nd Battalion of the 315th was awarded the Presidential Citation for this action as reported in all the world media. It is well documented in the "The Cross of Lorraine" (bibliog. 517). yet, cold and impersonal, this account can't even begin to touch the souls and feelings I have covered above in my Alsatian Confrontation." -- Joe Kane

Chapter Twelve – Part B
"Through the Window" - that fateful mortar round the day "Smitty" died in Bill Tilford's arms. Directly out of hell...at the lousy face of war!

Veteran Bill Tilford Sr. is the first-hand source for this next story. Originally called "That Day in Hatten", it is a fitting adjunct to Joe Kane's "Alsatian Confrontation." Bill's sons have worked tirelessly on publishing the full story, and this excerpt was written by his son Dave. It is truly a remarkable "F" Co. story. The connection they discovered to John Kane's story is astonishing:

"My dad, Bill Tilford, Sr. was a Pfc. In "F" Co., 315th Infantry. In the years since dad passed away in 1998, I have tried to locate some of the men he served with during WW2. I was unaware of the 315th Association until sometime in 2004 when my brother, Bill Jr., discovered it through the internet. After learning of the annual Reunions held by the 315th Association. I contacted Les Brantingham who invited me to attend the 2005 reunion in Cincinnati. I attended with my wife Sally and my brother, Bill Jr., but was unable to speak with anyone from "F" Co. while we were there.

I think it was in the Col. Boogie News following that 2005 reunion that I found a letter written by Joe Kane from Red Hook, NY. Joe's letter, which expressed his regrets for being unable to attend, was signed "Joe Kane", "F" Co. After reading Joe's letter I sent him a letter asking him if he knew or remembered my dad also in "F" Co.

When Joe responded a couple of weeks later, he did not mention if he knew dad, but he did send me a handwritten story about his experiences in the battle of Hatten. I will share a small part of Joe's story, but first it is important to share a story dad often told.

I remember hearing a lot of stories while growing up about dad's war experiences. He told me of basic training, his voyage overseas, landing in Italy and joining the 79th Div. as a replacement in France, his first combat was in Lauterbourg and many more. But the story that stands out in my memory over all others is one that took place in the Alsatian village of Hatten. 1945.

I remember those tears that would well up in his eyes when he told about his friend. Smith that he called "Smitty." Several men were holed in a cellar in a small house in Hatten. They were sitting in a circle trying to catch some rest as best they could. Dad told of the soldier that was sitting next to him reading the Stars and Stripes. (The US Army Newspaper)

For some reason that soldier, whom he never identified, stood up and handed the Stars and Stripes to Smitty who then sat down next to my dad. The moment Smitty sat down to read he was hit by shrapnel from a mortar round that came in through the cellar window!!! Smitty said, "Bill, I'm hit," fell to one side, and died in my dad's arms.

Death, of course, is no stranger to a combat soldier. It was all around them. This one though had a profound effect on my dad. I know all of his recounts of combat were painful and full of emotion, but it was obvious that this recount of "Smitty's death affected him more than any other. One can imagine how I felt when I read Joe Kanes' words. "Goosebumps" to say the least. Joe did not mention that he knew my dad, but one thing is for certain. Joe Kane was the soldier sitting next to my dad in the cellar, "That day in Hatten on" or about Jan. 12, 1945." -- Dave Tilford

Chapter Twelve – Part C
"The Day We Lost Baker Company" by Hub Ranger of Co. "A", 1st Battalion

"We're jumping off at 0700." That was the word First Sergeant Steel gave us in Co. Headquarters the previous evening. We'd heard such terse announcements before - from him or one of the platoon leaders. The leaders came and went as replacements. Only our company CO, Captain Harvey, and First Sergeant Steele seemed to survive while others didn't make it.

After being in a static position for four weeks we were ready for the worst. We'd faced it before on countless days across France and into some eastern provinces which we knew only as Alsace-Lorraine. I was the company radio operator and I replaced the original operator who had been killed by a sniper while standing in his shallow foxhole!

The next attack was against the fortified town of Scheibenhardt, 12/14/44, that turned out to be the anchor point of the Siegfried Line. It lasted a short day, got nowhere, and resulted in several killed and wounded. I saw my first Dragon's Teeth there... the anti-tank barriers! Although they looked fearful, they saved the lives of many American infantrymen who found cover from small arms fire in an attack when there was no other cover.

The bad news was we were attacking. The good news was our own Able Co. was being held in reserve & Baker Company was handling what we hoped was a routine attack. At 0700, 17 Jan. 1945, the radio was busy for half an hour or so as the Battalion got into position. We jumped off from Hoffen & Leiterswiller, a mile NNW of Rittershoffen. Baker Company passed through or around us as we huddled along the roadsides and listened to sporadic artillery coming and going in the vicinity.

Some armored units would have been reassuring, but none were assigned to us for the attack on this occasion. This another reason indicating they expected probable light resistance.

Baker Company was to attack the crossroads town of Rittershoffen!

This is directly down the road we were on coming from the northwest and leading southeast. As soon as they secured the town house by house, Able Co. was to move in behind them. Then Charlie Company was to come in from the southwest and occupy positions along the road coming from the next town to the east, Hatten, and that was it. It sounded quick and easy.

We watched the undersized Baker Company platoons passed by. Perhaps 70 or 80 men since they were down in strength due to casualties, from the full company of 150 men. For 2 hours we waited in the ditches along the road. We never saw or heard directly from Baker Co. again. That and the next day, and for weeks after! The news of what happened came back to us in pieces.

This is the story - Rescue Assault on Rittershoffen:

My radio went silent within 15 minutes after Baker Company passed through us. In anticipation of losing the radio or its operator, or both, we had made radio operators out of two riflemen in Able Co. We then placed a backpack radio, known as an SCR300 on each!

I talked with them in a quick radio check every half hour or so to make sure all sets or were OK. This was a strange malady that affected the SCR300 whenever it got exposed to the elements in a combat situation. My radio continued operating that day and saved a few lives as a result!

It became very silent, except for a few shells that came over night and day from single enemy guns that we called harassing fire. However, after two hours of this, we began getting battery fire. This usually meant that four guns would fire nearly simultaneously. In this case it was three guns from one enemy battery and four from two others.

This tells us that one gun in one battery was not operating for some reason. Hardly much encouragement. It also meant they knew something was coming or they would not have greatly increased their rate of fire. Two more hours went by and we finally got some indication of trouble! One lone GI came running back down the road from Rittershoffen. He was waving his arms and yelling at intervals, "Get those damn tanks up there! He said Baker Co. was cut off in a house and was taking point blank fire from a tank. We headed him back towards our Battalion HQ and waited for further orders. We thought he was a Baker Co. straggler, but never found out for sure. The official word came in another hour. Baker Company was cut off.

1st Battalion HQ decided, & Able Company was to attack to get them out. Charlie Co., it appeared, was pinned down in a field on the south west side of town. We formed two columns on the road and moved out towards Rittershoffen. As far as we knew, no enemy artillery observer could see, but about that time shells started battering the road every five or ten minutes.

The Battalion Commander came on the radio and asked for my Company Commander (CO). I said he wasn't around, and he said, "Find him, damn it." I asked the fellows up the road of me if they had seen him. They said he was up front looking over the situation. I passed the two forward scouts and went to a ridge separating us from town. It was getting very lonely when suddenly I saw a long line of tanks that none of us knew were there. Thankfully, they were ours. The CO was standing beside one of them and had the microphone of their radio on a long cord, talking to our Battalion CO. He chewed me out for being so far forward! "Ranger, if you keep this up you won't live long enough for us to send flowers to your funeral." Since none of the others who went before me got flowers, I didn't see how this applied, but I kept quiet and probably avoided a court martial.

I said I was only following the Battalion Commander's orders to find him. I headed back to the company and, as I started back down the road, I passed the first two scouts going in the other direction, I heard the enemy, three-gun battery go off. It was firing at a short range. I wrapped my arms around my head and seconds later the concussion lifted me, with my 55 lb. radio on my back, off of the ground a few inches and dropped me back down! I saw a red flash even though my eyes were closed. That is one way to tell a German shell from American. Theirs were red. Ours were yellow. I was sure I was hit. I wiggled one arm & one leg at a time. They all moved, and none fell off.

After a few minutes of no further shelling I stood up cautiously. There was an impressive hole 30 feet to my right, another in ditch to my left across the road, and another one 50 feet down the ditch near where the two scouts lay. I yelled to them, "Get up and move back until we get orders! They'll be shelling here again soon!" Neither of them moved.

I thought they were frozen with fear. They weren't. They were dead!!! Those German artillery men were good. They had fired from three to 5 miles away and put those shells in a diameter of about fifty to sixty feet. The frozen ground was our enemy that day. We couldn't dig holes and the ground absorbed less of the explosion from the shell. This sent shrapnel over a wider area, increasing its killing probability.

We moved back a few hundred yards, then got orders to attack across the triangular field to our right, past the tanks and go through a hedgerow of alder bushes & across another open field into the town. They gave us artillery. preparation, but fired back of the town for fear of hitting Baker Co. in case any of them were in the houses and still alive. No one knew for sure where they were!

The first platoon leader came back from talking to the CO. It was decided the first platoon would lead with the second and third following on their right and left. I was to go with the first platoon and the other two radiomen were to go with the second and third. We advanced toward the alders and that was the last of any organized attack.

The first platoon leader told me to stay on the hillside overlooking the town in case they got pinned down and needed artillery. As soon as the first soldiers passed through the alders mortar fire of various sizes started bursting all around. The three platoons were immediately pinned down by the mortars, & those who got beyond the alders were pinned down by small arms. The more aggressive riflemen crawled the three hundred yards toward the town. The CO wrote up some of those who made it, as heroes, for a Silver Star. They deserved it, but he told me later that they were simply crawling for cover. They knew their lives were numbered in minutes, in an open field with no cover, and nothing but bushes behind them. It looked safer in the foxholes they could see on the edge of town than in an open field.

The stalemate and disorganization resulted in further agitation by our CO to get tank support. but he didn't get them. We learned that we were passing through the 14th Armored Division that was being held in Army Reserve to be committed if a breakthrough was attempted. The Battle of the Bulge was going on north of us by about 100 miles,

The 14th Armored reluctantly gave us three tanks for a second attempt on the town. They were Shermans with 75mm cannons and 30 cal. machine guns. The lead tank got to the middle of the field and took a hit from an anti-tank gun, breaking a tread, but doing no other damage. The other two tanks turned back.

On my radio I heard one of our riflemen, carrying the spare radio, and lying in the alders. They said that the crew had tried to bail out twice, but they were driven back by small arms fire. They tried a white handkerchief waved out the driver's hatch but got another surge of fire when they started to climb out.

Mortars were coming closer. Whereas small mortars could be survived inside the tank, they might set it on fire... the thing tankers fear most. I called Battalion and asked for some smoke shells. The first battery fire of four smoke shells was fired at three-minute intervals. There was a fairly stiff wind and the smoke was blowing away before the tankers could get out.

I told the man on the radio and he suggested doubling the fire rate. I agreed. It worked & the tankers wisely jumped out and ran for the bushes. The whole crew made it. About that time, I noted that our company headquarters had been set up by Sergeant Steele in holes under some apple trees a few dozen yards away across the hill from me. I thought this was a poor place, but there were no other holes. I was sharing a foxhole with two 14th Armored infantrymen. Mortar shells were landing around us.

Everyone in our company headquarters was above ground during a relatively quiet period when a shell hit in the apple tree right over their heads - an air burst! It was a small shell and the only effect was that the first sergeant got a nick in the back of his neck. One of the runners looked at his wound and found a small scratch that didn't even need a band-aid.

By now, 0700 morning attack, had become a 1400-hour attack. The lack of progress on our part used up another two or three hours. It was late afternoon and just starting to get dark on a heavily overcast day. At that time, I was in a foxhole waiting for orders and felt a shudder in the ground. I looked out to see an unexploded mortar shell lying on its side 60 feet from my hole.

As I stared at it the color appeared to be olive drab. I thought I could see three yellow stripes around the tube just back of the small body where the propellant charge was housed. I looked at it more closely through my binoculars and saw it was a U.S 81 mm. shell. later I walked over to it and found that it had not exploded because the second safety pin had not been pulled out. It was obvious that the Germans did not know how to arm the U.S 81 mm. shell!

On and off all day we had heard explosions that sounded like U.S. weapons being fired at us. Some of the fellows trying to crawl across the field into Rittershoffen reported later hearing 50 caliber machine guns firing at them. That was an American weapon only, and it had a very distinctive sound. We found out the next day that an American unit had been attacked in the town.

Then they abandoned some of their weapons and ammunition. It must have been a heavy weapons company because that was the kind being fired at us.

As darkness descended we got the word to pull back to the west while the 14th Armored Division stayed in place. I watched German artillery explode progressively closer to the tank retriever that was towing away one of the stalled or damaged, Shermans!

It was not possible for artillery fire to be controlled by an observer from anything we could see, Yet the shells kept bursting closer as each series on rounds from the 3-gun battery continued. The retriever was a moving target and the closest and last shell hit about 30 feet behind the tank being towed behind it.

The retriever was buttoned up & and the crew may have never known the close call they had since their periscopes could not look backward. They disappeared… over the brow of a hill just as the last shell missed them, and we relaxed again.

My Able Company moved into houses in Rittershoffen. Of the 90 men in Able Co. who started out that morning we could find about 15!

Baker Company consisted of the one possible straggler who came by us yelling for tanks. We heard they sedated him at the 1st Battalion Aid station and evacuated him to a hospital. He was incoherent all of the time until he passed out!

The tanks crew said they bailed out of their tank after the tread was blown off but were pinned down in it until a smoke screen was laid down in front of them. The Able Co. fellow with me told them I was responsible for it. They shook my hand and said it saved their lives. The tank commander said he was putting me in for a Silver Star, but it was about ten years before I received recognition, and then it was the Bronze Star.

We ate cold K-rations and slept until daylight, the morning of 18 January. We got word we were to assemble for a truck move. About half of Able Company have been rounded up. The word from the few who got across the field in the attack on Rittershoffen, and then pulled back when no one joined them, was that they had a few men surrendering near a pillbox in town.

They also knew of a number of casualties. They also learned that Baker Company got into the first three houses. The attacking tank came up to their building, put the 88mm gun into a window and fired. The house collapsed on everyone in it!

The two platoons in the other two adjacent houses, including Baker Co. HQ group, then surrendered and were marched east and south of the town presumably towards a POW processing area. Baker Company was no more.

It had become the victim of poor reconnaissance, poor deployment, and an aggressive enemy. The only anti-tank weapons they had available were several bazookas. Those were of little use against tanks in a congested village. No tanks or tank destroyers were allowed to accompany them. The tanks were being held in reserve in case of a breakthrough.

This did occur in the Battle of the Bulge area. The aggressive combination of getting into Rittershoffen too fast, with no support, except for artillery, was a fatal combination. Our artillery was of little use after Baker Company was cut off in the village without radio communications. Our artillery fire control did not know which houses U.S. troops occupied.

A member of Able Company who was hiding in an air raid shelter told me he heard a German soldier outside talking to captured members of Baker company, offering them candy, so we knew at least some were taken prisoner. (HW edit 3/18/08: These turned out to be the "Eighty Valliant MIA's of Baker Co.") -- Hub Ranger

Chapter Twelve - Part D
The Tale of the Stockless BAR, by H. West

Among the vignettes of Baker Company is the tale of the "Stockless BAR" (Browning Automatic Rifle) that just won't quit. With unquenchable spirit it just kept firing... stock or no stock. This saga has its origins in the section dealing with the story... "The shot that changes my life".

It involves my vertical foxhole, so confined that there is no room in it for my BAR. It is during the wee hrs. of 15 Jan. amidst a horrendous artillery barrage, starting about 0130 hrs. The saga quickly goes downhill from there!

About 0130 hrs. I finally whack and chip through the frozen crust and scrape out a vertical hole (not horizontal) barely big enough to get my feet into, and barely deep enough, in a twisted crouch, to get my steel helmet just below the parapet rim. There is no room for my Browning Automatic Rifle (BAR).

It is either me or the BAR to go in the hole, but not both. The BAR loses and goes horizontal, up on the rim. A few hours later at about 0400 hrs. the sheer, nerve rattling concussion and a large jagged piece of shrapnel from one of these artillery shells blows the stock off my BAR.

This leaves a very ugly, ragged, black plastic butt end. The shrapnel zinged by, just inches above his helmeted head. The BAR had been resting on the rim of my vertical foxhole. Thus my unique "Stockless BAR" is born... still shoots like hell from the hip... and is clearly looking for adventure!

And wow! It gets more than it bargained for, with two owners in two corners of pure hell, at the lousy face of war.

It is 15 January1945. These are tough times and the temperature is near zero. On a frozen white mountain north of Reipertswiller in the Northern Alsace Vosges. This story starts to unfold. It is amidst a horrendous, two-three-hour, nighttime, incoming artillery barrage. This mayhem blows the stock off the BAR!

Six hours later, after the first owner, Pfc. Harrison West is hit by a sniper & on his way down the mountain, the second owner, Pfc. Donald Weiskopff, had been my assistant on the BAR team. Now for sure Weiskopff is the BAR man in the spotlight ''front and center!" Our 2nd Squad leader, Gerry Cone, sidles over to him and says. "Weiskopff, go out there and retrieve West's BAR." It is resting on the frozen white mountain, exactly where I dropped it the instant I was hit. Now my "Stockless BAR" is still looking for adventure!

It mused, "This is a sad, lonely posture in which to end it all for WW2... This fate simply cannot be allowed to stand." The stockless weapon is right, but it will take all the men, and all the fire power in the 2nd Platoon to enable its rescue. Weiskopff comes back, "Cone, no way... you are out of your gourd.

West nearly got his head blown off out there. You are crazy! But Weiskopff is game and has the courage to comply. He crawls under the loud, thunderous staccato... under an unbelievable of hail of suppression fire, retrieves the BAR minus stock. He fires it all the way into the town of Rittershoffen two days later, on 17 Jan. So is that my "Stockless BAR" is off on its second adventure. Concurrently on 17 Jan, I am headed south on the Hospital Train.

Dateline: 17 January 1945, Hoffen, 2 mi. NW of Rittershoffen.

This in the middle of the horrific, 12-day Battle of Hatten and Rittershoffen. We pick up this saga on the heels of the firsthand account of Sgt. Hub Ranger, above. We start with Hub's words: Baker Company was no more. This is for sure; behold below.

National Personnel Records Center

Military Personnel Records (MPR) Page Ave., St. Louis, MO

***Dateline*: October 21-25, 2002**

It is a busy morning in the Research Room at MPR, Oct. 23. Perched on a special, rolling, research chair, my eyes are glued to a remarkable, microfilm "time machine," a special screen with unique controls. I am looking at the Morning Report of 21 Jan.1945. Hopefully searching the raw text of the report, I am hoping to find more than just words about my buddies. These are the GI"s of Baker Company who vanished on Jan. 17. The clerk who typed the text says there is a roster, and my anticipation reaches a crescendo. A few clicks later and on the screen right in front of my eyeballs is a beautiful roster: The classification of the following named EM (enlisted men) is changed from "Duty" to MIA (Missing in Action) as of 21 Jan. 1945.

Thus, comes to light for all in the 315th a full roster, numbered 1-80, listing the FID (Field Ident. No.) No. 1-80, ASN (Army Serial Number/ Dog Tag), Last Name, First Name, MOS (Military Occupational Specialty, Rank, Platoon, Status (confirmed POW [Prisoner of War], dead KIA [Killed in Action] or alive.

Of the 80 Valliant MIA's, the following of immediate personal interest:

No.9 - S Sgt. Gerald K. Cone, POW; No.14 - Sgt. Samuel E Hayes, POW; No.42 -T Sgt. Robert M Nixon, POW; No.46 - Pvt. Pagan A. Pedro, Status Unknown (This could well be my buddy "Mexico."); and last, but not least, No.77 - Pre. Donald A. Weiskopff, alive to tell his story in 2002, 2003 on DVD.

I did not pull up the Officer's roster but one, Lt. Howard D Hull, Jr. is also alive to tell his story in 2002, 2003 on DVD, and in Louisville in 2007!

***Dateline*: Wed., January 17, 0700 hrs., Hoffen, 2 miles NE of Rittershoffen.**

At 0700 the men of Baker Company jump off. The long column is a sad sight. The undersized Baker platoons pass by Able Company, idle at roadside. The sharp eyes of Able Company no doubt cannot miss one strange guy in the long. Baker column... he was carrying a fearsome BAR without that typical bipod, usually seen in WW2 movies whirling around the barrel when held high.

There is something else missing from this guy's BAR. Most of its black, plastic stock is gone. What is left to be seen is only a small remaining segment of ugly fearsome, jagged and fractured, black plastic. This is just behind the "pistol grip," the metal trigger housing and the receiver.

Our Able Company guys behold a sight quite out of the ordinary. It is brand new BAR man, Don Weiskopff, with his stockless BAR. You will recall that the "Stockless BAR" is still looking for adventure. And my successor Don Weiskopff is about to accommodate this spirited weapon, big time! Surely by 0800 hrs. Cone, Hayes, Weiskopff, and Hull move into 1 of the 3 northern most houses in town.

Don plus the fearsome "Stockless BAR". The bunch is lined up outside and now the obvious predicament is at hand. No way can Don manage this bunch of POWs by himself without Baker Co. support. And this help was simply not forthcoming. The reason is even more graphic and sad. As Hub Ranger points out, when reviewing large blowups of the maps... bulk of Baker Company "disappears" in the cellars of those first three houses!

They had no choice. Ordinarily, the cellars would have been a reasonably safe place to hide. But not so with the lousy Nazi bastards in control of the town. German tanks arrive on the scene, unchallenged by any US 7th Army tanks, stick the muzzles of their 88mm guns directly in the cellar windows and fire point blank.

Then, for added measure, their flame throwing tanks arrive. They stick their deadly "fire squinters" in the same windows and, point blank, simply incinerate any remaining Baker survivors. All this happens long before Able Company arrives in Rittershoffen.

CHAPTER THIRTEEN

Hospital evacuation train after wound...
From 1st Battalion Aid Station and MASH
through Besancon and Marseilles

P REFACE REMARKS: The action timeline for this chapter covers the period 11 November 1944 through 15 January 1945. The primary source documents are war letters written 63 years ago.

Chapter Thirteen - Part A
Hospital Evacuation Train. Looking up into the eyes of Madelene Carroll. 46th General Hospital, Besancon, France
Dateline: **22 Jan. 1945, only 7 days after I was hit!**

Following my classic, snow sled descent down the Reipertswiller mountain it took me six steps to arrive at the starting point for the interlude saga unfolding below. Starting off with the 1st Battalion Aid Station and MASH surgery, these steps covered the entire, hospital evacuation route, via ambulance, south from Lichtenberg, through Haguenau to Strasbourg.

Here we boarded a 14 car US Army hospital evacuation train, further south to Besonson, France, near the Swiss border, where our story begins. For a nineteen-year-old kid it really blew my mind... an absolutely unforgettable experience!!!

Holy smoke! Who was that chick that just breezed down the aisle??? I was now prepared to accept most anything in the way of Army nurses and Red Cross gals. I had come out of my MASH neck operation to find I had nearly pulverized the 'o-so soft hand of a straight double for Priscilla Lane! I had been getting along swell back at the Field Hospital with brunette not unlike Ann Rutherford.

But now!! That blonde Red Cross girl who just went down the aisle of this Hospital Train---Holy smoke! She was just too-too. I tell you, there is something fishy around here… They just don't come like that. My eyes got big as I poked my nose out from under the GI blanket and busted neck or no busted neck, followed her all the way down the car!

She caught my eye and said, "Hello soldier." I just gulped, almost expired, and waited for her to come back with her basket of cookies full. I still think there is something 'fishy' around here, so I Shanghai'd her and the next time 'chawed' on a cookie and got to talking with her… found out a little bit about the classiest gal in the 1945 public eye… no contest!!

She was a regular Red Cross girl, like all the rest, working where she was told to. She is currently assigned to this 14-car train to the delight of all 224 wounded GI's aboard. The most radiant, cheerful personality I had yet known. She had given up a lot in the States, over here on her own hook, she was doing a great job helping battered and shredded GI's forget their misery! Yes, all of you in the States know her too. Her name? Madeleine Carroll, classy lady of Stage and Screen!!

Chapter Thirteen - Part B
46th General Hospital, Besancon, France
Dateline: **22 January 1945, A Snapshot of the Main Hospital Ward.**

Forgive me for mentioning it… but I find the atmosphere here so apart from that snowy wooded mountain where I was hit, that it may be likened to snatching Yahooty from the foaming jaws of Hell on Earth and elevating him to the heights of Shangri-La! This, all at the snarling crack of a Nazi schmeiser sniper rifle.

Here, amidst the melodious strains of "New World Symphony," "The Blue Danube Waltz," Artie Shaw's Beguine and Glen Miller's "In The Mood" Incredulous GI's relax their battle-weary bodies in soft, clean, warm, beds and close their eyes in vain efforts to conceive fully, just what has come to pass in the last few days.

This soldier's mind wanders back to the glare and heat of the lights in surgery, to the soft, cool, refreshing sweep of the nurses wash cloth over his brow. He winced slightly as he gazed up into the eyes of an angel… she was kidding him about his mustache and threatened to cut it off… but the protests were too evident! He felt like a bad boy who has been playing in the mud as she scrubbed violently at his hands without the slightest effect.

By her soft reassuring voice, he knew the worst was over -- the storm had passed and… new rays of peace, quiet and rest filtered through a clearing sky. And as the stretcher was lifted from the MASH operating table he felt strangely like the man on the flying carpet! Thus, it was that he was floated back to the ward, that wonderful angel still by his side.

His eyes became fixed on his buddies all around him, some all but tied in a bow knot with casts, braces, rubber hoses & bandages. Very few were moaning & groaning... yet all with adequate cause. They were too overwhelmed by the treatment they were being given.

Above the row after row of hospital cots there were strung tension wires like the clothes lines in Mom's backyard. Down these tension wires... like birds on power lines staggered row after row of bottles. These contained plasma, life giving whole blood, and the clear fluid used for intravenous feeding. Nurses and ward boys moved quickly about periodically to check temperatures and blood pressures. The slightest deviations from normal would bring the entire staff to the bedside of one patient. For those who were able to eat, hot steaming trays were brought... to others liquid and soft diets as required.

The hot broth would flow down to the tips of their toes; for practically all guys it was the first time their feet had been warm and dry in so long it hurt to think about it! And it was their first warm decent meal in months! For this soldier it is first week after he was hit. During the long nights there is one thing he will never forget... that high monotone moan of a French Alsace girl way down at the other end of the ward. She had been walking down the street with a GI near the front. A Nazi 88 mm shell came in and blew her leg off. Killed the GI!!

Some time ago my name was put on an evacuation list to be shipped further back to the rear. The other day the transportation arrived, and this soldier went prancing out of the ward fully dressed - all decked out in combat boots and a shiny 79th Div. patch.

I walked up to the ambulance, and I'll be darned if they didn't put me on a stretcher! After I had been walking around for a week, I didn't argue. Stretcher patients get better treatment on evacuation trains.

Chapter Thirteen - Part C
235th General Hospital in Marseilles... A whole new look

I'm now at my destination 235th General Hospital in balmy Marseilles, now well settled in my new ward, surpassing anything I might have dreamed of! For all the gentle, warm breeze, fresh air and sunshine, I might as well have stepped off the train in Miami Florida.

The ambulance driver checked over our records at the receiving office and shortly we rolled up in front of a row of neat, trim, modern bungalows. These wards were small, simple and clean... This place is strangely apart from war. The permanent buildings are laid out under a magnificent array of glistening red tile roofs.

A grand court with its stucco walls standing as an excuse for vines to grow and enclosing a tiny city within itself. Not far away, a spring-fed swimming pool, no less! We were lucky, my buddy and I, taking the last two beds left, at the end of ward, right across from the nurse's office, next to the kitchen and supply room. So, Joe and I really got it made... a cozy little room all to ourselves... twin beds, a small table and chairs, and real electric light.

There is no darn battle ax ward Sgt. here, so any time we want we can walk into the kitchen and guzzle down all the juices, peaches cookies and cake we want. Yeah, this the real deal. I am sure thankful for the rest it will give me! So far, they have not tried to tie my neck in a knot, like in Besancon. I have my fingers crossed ... maybe they will leave me alone!

Chapter Thirteen - Part D
Projects for Red Cross Building, Special Services

All of this facility and infrastructure improvement need carpentry work of every possible description. These needs, listed by unit are:

Hospital Wards - Tray racks, benches, stools, desks, tables & shelves.

Admin. Offices - "in-out" boxes, wastepaper baskets, shelves,

Red Cross Bldg. &, Special Services - Lawn Chairs, Coffee Tables, Bulletin Boards, Sign Boards, Posters.

Chapter Thirteen - Part E
All leather pouch for BAR ammo

I began working for the Red Cross... Made myself a splendid, all leather, BAR ammo and K-Ration pouch for my web belt. My bet it would sell for $5-$10 in the States. It resembles an expensive looking press photographer bag with convenient buckles and flaps, with hand stitching all over the thing!

The Red Cross had all the needed leather, but it was much too thick and had to be planed down to 3/32" They also supplied the rivets, tools, drills, needles and heavy thread needed. I salvaged the big buckles, and eyelets from a pair of GI Combat boots. It really turned out nice, but now every RC gal and nurse in the whole darn Hospital wants me to make them one like it! Wow, that's a lot of work!

Chapter Thirteen - Part F
POW capture in Alsace - Labor for workshop

He was coming towards me with his hands behind his head. The muzzle of my BAR at hip-fringing position was right on him.

He was visibly trembling all over, "Nicht scheissen… Nicht scheisson," over and over again, he stammered and whined. I looked him straight in the eye with what must have been a terrible look, as I was tired, bitter, and downright mad… I told him to get the hell on back to the rear and followed him for some distance as he passed by, pivoting my BAR like a turret gun!

Chapter Thirteen - Part G
Lawn chair production line in workshop

Now the confounding part of this story. To help me out on whatever job I might be working on in the carpenter shop, I was assigned one permanent POW. Every morning I would go up to the Stockade and sign him out., then every evening I would check him back in. We'll call our "permanent POW" Heinrich Bauer (not his real name).

He was a young fella, 19, from a small town near (population 25,000) near Kassel, Germany. He was about 5'10" of average build, with the bright face of a kid about 15. His dad employed about a dozen men in a small cabinet making business. He had a cute kid sister 10, and another about 20. He entered the Army when he was 17 ½ years old. After basic training he entered the combat engineers, stationed in Bordeaux, France, for a couple of years, and was captured in Alsace in December 1944.

While working with him I got to know him quite well. He didn't take after his dad, as he was a little dumb as a carpenter. Once I caught him, sweating profusely, after he badly ripped all the way down a 20 ft, 3/4-inch plank with a crosscut saw!!! This, while a very sharp rip saw was lying on the bench, unused!!!

I almost couldn't believe it at first, but I set him straight on the key difference between crosscut (quere-schnit) and rip saw (trench schnit). From then on, he learned very fast, and determined the most efficient procedure at each stage in the lawn chair assembly process.

On the whole, these POW's are darn good craftsmen. Give them a job and they will build anything! We had one group of 4 in the shop once who were really professional carpenters in civilian life. Heinrich thought the world of me because of the way I set up the line, with so darn many chairs coming off it! That kid was a hard worker. There must have been a full 125 yards of rip sawing to do in each of those 20 chairs.

Somehow, I got myself contracted with the Red Cross to produce some 20 odd, 34-part, lawn or deck chairs from an original design. These are for the Red Cross and Officers' living quarters. There was only one thing to do: set up a regular, 6 stage assembly line and run the darn things off in mass production. I standardized 11 different parts and patterns, and started piling up stacks of numbered parts, with the help of a few German POW's ...all with hand saws! To be made right, screws were required, but we had to substitute with nails.

Chapter Thirteen - Part H
235th General... Medical Review Board SHAEF G2 Document Section, Versailles Palace. Discharged from 235th Gen. with Limited Assignment. 3/19-25 - Transport north to Versailles. 3/26 - Start new job with Eisenhower's SHAEF Main HQ

In my last NL I wrote of an abrupt change from previous notes that I probably would be going back to the combat front. A group of Officers from the 235th Medical Staff reviewed for me the Medical Record to date, starting with the details of the neck operation in the field MASH 1/16/45.

They said they had no idea of the long-term implications of everything tied off in my neck. They then asked me what skills I had to guide them in structuring a non-combat, limited assignment? My quick reply was "I can type like the dickens!" So, it was that they "boarded" me for job with Eisenhower' SHAEF Main HQ. I was reclassified with a 405 MOS (Military Occupational Specialty).

Chapter Thirteen - Part I
235th General Hospital... Excursion into Marseilles.
The Depot-Finee!!! A one-day saga...
Dateline: **March 18 1945**

"Depot - Finee!" "Depot - Fineee!???" You crazy louse, you - you can't wind up this busted down trolley for the night!!! Now looka here Pop (the trolley conductor)- stop jabberin' for a minute... How am I supposed to know which one of these chattering, clattering street cars goes to where I want to go!!??

Here I am, way out on the opposite side of Marseilles from the Hospital. I am a soldier patient, Pop, and you have got to get me back home to my hospital! What?? You don't speak German! Well, you crazy fool, I don't speak French, and that puts both in deep water!

But if you holler "Depot Fineee" just once more, your company is going to lose a good man! Now don't you see, Pop ... No compree, no compree! So here I was, blowing my top at the trolley conductor as the trolley conductor just as the streetcar turned off the main line into its final destination Depot in the middle of Lord knows where in Marseilles.

He clanged the bell for the last time and made it clear to all passengers that it was time to get off so the trolley could go to sleep for the night! All I could think of was the American Red Cross. All the Frenchmen could think of was the American MPs (Military Police).

I didn't like to think about the latter as it seems I was without certain, key slip of key paper, called a legal pass off the Hospital Base. So, this soldier was on very shaky ground... AWOL (absent without leave) but with a strong case of "Cabin Fever!" Very early this morning, it seems I had escaped the base confines by going through a hole in the fence!!!

Bewildered, I crossed the street from the Trolley Depot to a busy Pub. The guys there quickly realized my predicament and phoned the American Red Cross in Marseilles. The gal there dropped everything, drove halfway across town, and picked me up in her own personal car, and took me back to the same hole in the fence from which I had escaped. The 235th Gen. Hosp. staff never missed me, and thanks to my savior, the Red Cross gal, the AWOL charge never went on my military record!

CHAPTER FOURTEEN

Eisenhower's Military Intelligence Service (a whole new life at SHAEF MAIN HQ)

G-2 Doc. Sect, At Versailles, France & Frankfurt, Germany

PREFACE REMARKS: The action timeline for this chapter covers the Months of April & May 1945. The primary source documents are war letters written 63 years ago.

They "boarded" me for a job with Eisenhower' SHAEF Main HQ I was reclassified with a 405 MOS.

Chapter Fourteen - Part A
Petite ecurie (small horse stables) of the Grand Palace; while working for G2 doc sect. cobwebs in ears - straw in hair. SHAEF Main HQ, Versailles, France... just west of Paris.
Dateline: **3 April 1945, 0615 hours**

I still have cobwebs in my ears, and straw in my hair. My combat watch is ticking... the second sweep hand still ticking. It says 0615 hours, 3 April 1945. I roll over once again on my real-for-sure straw bunk trying to get the straw out of my mouth, and then I recall, (small horse stables) of the Grand Palace...

The last night, after the long train and truck ride from the 235th 45th General Hospital, I found myself in the Petite Ecurie (small horse stables) of the Grand Palace of Versailles where Napoleon of a century past kept his prize horses. I don't know how his horses made out.

To heck with my problem with the straw. All we Americans need to put our own personal "bummers" in a perspective. I roll out of the straw sack and hit the chow line. This my first day on the job working for Gen. Eisenhower, and I am really excited at the prospect...

Chapter Fourteen - Part B
Grand Ecurie (large horse stables) of the Grand Palace; In the vaulted opulence, in an ageless stone building

Our daily "Workplace" of G2 Doc Section. I walk across the vast entry courtyard of the Grand Palace of Versailles from the Petite Ecurie to the Grand Ecurie, entering the vaulted opulence of the ageless stone building the sign says, "Supreme Headquarters, Allied Expeditionary Force (SHAEF), Main." There is a SHAEF Rear in England, and a SHAEF Forward in Reims. Napoleon is surely aghast!!!

Chapter Fourteen - Part C
The functions & staff of G2 Documents, Introduction to Chief Clerk, Banks

I climb to the second floor amidst a hot bed and hustle of American, British, Canadian and French Uniforms... all in vigorous motion. It is a tripartite, Allied Headquarters, and it is clear that a war is going on. Halfway down the long hall I spot this sign, "G2 Document Section." The "G" indicates, in this case, the highest level of HQ. "S" for example is for lower levels... Regimental and below. The "2" indicates the military staff function: G1- Personnel, G2- Intelligence, G3-Plans and Operations, and GS- Supply. I sort of expect to meet Ike (Eisenhower) somewhere down the hall, but alas, it is not to be. He is busy elsewhere!

I enter the portal of the G2 Document Section and immediately I am surrounded by the resounding clatter of typewriters, mimeograph machines, teletype machines, all punctuated by phones ringing off the hook.

Over in the corner is a distinguished British Sgt., perhaps about 25 years old, in his soft, fuzzy, brown-gray uniform, with absolutely huge stripes, picks up the phone and answers loudly amidst the chaos: "Chief Clucks Office... Banks speaking."

I am to hear this perhaps a couple thousand times from Sgt. Banks in my SHAEF career. It takes me the better part of a week to figure out just what a "Cluck" is, and what were all the "clucks" doing here anyway??? It turns out: "Cluck" is the British Cockney accent for USA "Clerk." Banks is clearly not an "Eastender," but neither is he from the Oxford aristocracy (typical of practically all of the British Officers).

Chapter Fourteen - Part D
The basic functions of G2 documents. Introduction to American
Master Sgt. Ed Wall, my boss for the next year in the ETO

Next to Banks, behind a mammoth double desk, flanked on all sides by arrays of in-out boxes, sits American Master Sgt. Ed Wall, my boss for the next year in the ETO. Perhaps in his late twenties, Ed has a perky, round face this exudes energy and confidence. I sound out, "Pfc. Harrison West reporting for duty!" My paperwork having preceded me, his face lights up with a big, expectant smile, "Welcome aboard!"

I am the first limited-assignment combat GI to arrive in his office via the general hospital system! From the very beginning I am extended marvelous courtesy and sort of unspoken quiet support. Ed enlightens me on what all the "clucks" are doing, but still doesn't tell me what they are. He explains that the Intelligence Section is perhaps ninety percent German speaking. It is staffed by about a hundred, including a total of about eight intelligence officers (pretty well split between Brits and American).

The prime function of G2 Document Section is to receive a bewildering flood of German military and governmental documents, dug up by the chain of field operatives and free French all over the ETO.

Further, the Section classifies, translates and analyzes archives and microfilms. and then distributes the distilled data to all corners of the SHEAF Command and Military Units. After VE day these documents are literally dug up from a vast network of salt mines all over Germany where Hitler's henchmen had stashed them. There are two non-coms (Non-commissioned Officers) involved here: Master Sgt. Ed Wall and Tech Sgt. Carl Maes, the latter from Green Bay, Wisconsin, my two bosses for the next year in the ETO.

Chapter Fourteen - Part E
Introduction to American Sgt. Carl Maes. my immediate
supervisor and originator of the Tag "Sunshine Soldier"

Sgt. Ed Wall next introduces me to Carl who issues a huge grin from a magnificent, chiseled face, with American like features. What a guy. Later on, in Frankfurt am Main, Germany, Carl is to give me the nickname "Sunshine," a tag which is to stick, and of which I shall be eternally proud.

Both Ed and Carl are about eight years older than I, really above draft age. They are both obviously seasoned business school graduates recruited from these schools or business in the States. Ed Wall is, no contest, the fastest touch typist I have ever seen, before or since!!!

Chapter Fourteen - Part F
Introduction to the fuzzy uniformed British (Brits)

In the back of the G2 Documents Room. It is now 0830 hours and Carl takes me back to my desk in the back of the room, one wall away from the windows, is flanked by a solid row of personal lockers and supply cabinets. The only American in sight, I am located smack in the middle of a phalanx of four fuzzy British uniforms. Eastenders all, they surely are the "Magnificent Four!" They treat me with a special respect and sensitivity.

Let's get back to the magnificent British and the Eastenders of yesteryear. Carl Maes shows me my new Underwood Standard typewriter and pulls all the needed supplies to get me going with my new job. I am pretty well settled in on my first assignment.

Chapter Fourteen – Part G
Everything stops for traditional British tea time

"Aye Matey... it's tay time! Where's yur moog??"

Before I can get in gear for anything, I notice that all of the normal typewriter and teletype clatter has abruptly stopped and replaced by determined footsteps. It seems that every British enlisted man in the room along with British Major Dogwood, (who happened to be caught wandering around the room at 1000 hours) is now in a herd; in a hell-bent dash for a neat row of lockers on the side of the room!!!

Then abruptly over my left shoulder I hear one of my newfound Eastender friends, his voice coming through, loud and clear.

"Aye Matey ... it's tay time!" Somewhat alarmed, my brain is studiously trying to function... what in the name of heaven is "tay?"

Before I can respond he comes back, "Where's yur moog?? If ya ain't got your moog, ya caint 'av yur tay!"

Now I really have problems. I'm not at all sure if "moogs" are part of the regular fare issued to American GI's... even if I had a single clue as to what they were. My local friend grabs my hand and tugs me along. His locker swings open to reveal three shiny "moogs" hanging on their special hooks. There is one he has specially washed for me, and one extra... heaven forbid, that we should run out of serviceable "moogs!"

So it is that I am baptized into the solid British tradition of morning tea time. I am never able to get the American Quartermaster to issue me a moog. But I do go out and buy an American Style mug of proper capacity to replace the moog loaned.

AFTERWORD -- BY NANCY WINTER WEST

My husband Harrison handed me this book shortly before he passed away March 11, 2015. He told me it was finished. We later found abstracts for additional chapters he may have intended to write at one time. They summarize the many more remarkable experiences he had after VE day.

The book closes as he begins his assignment with Eisenhower's military intelligence service in the aftermath of the war. Working with allies from Britain and the USA, he helped organize maps, charts, and documents that had been hidden in salt mines by the Germans during the war. The British tea he recalls at the close was one of the many memorable moments he enjoyed meeting people from around the world. He took a furlough in the French Riviera, and saw more USO shows with Bob Hope, Jack Benny, Ingrid Bergman and other Hollywood stars of the day. He also wrestled with difficult emotions as he and his fellow soldiers pieced together everything that had happened.

One of the last things he did before returning home was to go around Berlin buying cameras – an early glimpse of his lifelong passion for photography. He packed them all up to ship home. He vividly recalled his parents greeting him at the dock in New York.

From the moment he reported for induction to the time he returned to the USA in the spring of 1946, his entire wartime experience had lasted around 3 years –years that shaped the man he would become. He was awarded a Certificate of Merit and promotion for his initiative, high attention to detail and diligence in his documentation work. Our family would admire these same character qualities in Harrison his whole life. He was awarded the Purple Heart for the shot he survived, but the emotional scars were far deeper than the one on his throat. Like most of his fellow soldiers, he quietly put the trauma of his combat experiences in the past. They would resurface fifty years later with a fury.

He returned to his studies at Purdue University on the GI Bill, studying mechanical engineering. He was a leader on campus with his fraternity, and in the Purdue Student Union. This is where we met. Serving together on the Union Board, we soon found ourselves dating and riding around campus on his motor scooter named Maxi. We married as he was finishing his engineering degree, and I was finishing my early childhood education degree.

He landed a great job with General Electric in Cincinnati, designing jet engines. We raised six wonderful children and 12 awesome grandchildren together. We made a great team. He always seemed determined to live for all his war buddies who did not return. He started a July Fourth parade in our hometown, an event that began on our front lawn and driveway and continues to this day, a wonderful community-wide event in Wyoming, Ohio. To ensure his children knew and appreciated the wonderful country he and his friends fought to keep free, we used his GE vacation every year for road trips to our national parks. He diligently documented those trips with his camera, photos we all enjoy to this day. His creativity and attention to detail shone in the wonderful things he built for and with our family in his workshop.

The earliest effect of his war memories was discovering that singing in church was too emotional for him. It stirred memories of the fear he felt in the MASH hospital - that he might not ever sing or speak again. But it was not until the televised events of the Gulf War and the 50th anniversary of D-Day that the full battle memories seemed to come flooding back to him. He experienced intense post-traumatic stress and vivid flashbacks. It became his mission to write this book. His research was relentless, including several trips to the National Archives.

He also spent time revisiting his original letters written to his parents during the war. These letters also provided an enormous wealth of information and stories, told in his own words as a 19-year-old soldier.

For the first time ever, he got involved with the annual reunion of his military group, the 315th regiment of the "Fighting 79th" Combat Infantry Division. We both enjoyed getting to know these people from around the country. They were all from different walks of life, but their time serving as teenage soldiers together created a lifetime bond. Telling their stories to one another was therapeutic, and we recorded many of these stories on video. Getting together with his fellow soldiers each year and corresponding between reunions helped Harrison tremendously to make sense of his war experience.

Finally, Harrison decided that returning to France would be the ultimate way to finish filling in the gaps. With children and grandchildren along, we took a remarkable trip back to many of the villages he and his fellow soldiers helped liberate. It was extraordinary. We will never forget the warm welcome of the French people, and the gratitude they expressed to Harrison and his friends who were not able to return. That trip and another with his regiment finally brought him peace.

None of us will ever be able to comprehend what those teenage soldiers experienced. Harrison did his best to describe it in his original letters home, and in this book of reflections decades later. The message he repeated to his family was "The price of freedom is eternal vigilance." He wanted to make sure future generations never forget that freedom cannot be taken for granted.

A wonderful quote from his original war letters sums up Harrison's sunny optimism: "Gee, it's nice to know that through all this cold, dank mud and mist that is today, there looms a tomorrow so bright it cannot be fully conceived in our infantile minds." This bright outlook earned him the nickname Sunshine. No matter what he faced, he always found creative solutions and a way to see things positively.

Harrison was an extraordinary soldier, citizen, son, husband, father and grandfather. I hope future generations will read this and remember the positive spirit and message of our "Sunshine Soldier."

Nancy "Pinky" West